Falling From The Sky

By Captain Will Smith

Dedications:

- To my father who I never had a chance to say goodbye to.

- My mom for being my backbone.

- Larry for being brave enough to never stop.

- And my two sons for always loving me and never judging me.

Foreword:

The first time I met Will, we dug a ditch together. He showed up early for the job with shovel in hand, a smile on his face, and a sheen of sweat already glossing his forehead from the Florida heat. His clothes were simple and neat; not the nearly ruined shirt and pants a typical contract laborer might wear for a gig like this. I called him last minute.

It was the fall of 2003, and I was pursuing my dream of building a custom home construction company. My first job was a good-sized room addition. Optimistically I ordered the concrete to be poured on Monday morning. But here it was Friday afternoon and no one had shown up to dig the trenches. It was too late to call the concrete off—I had paid for it and it was going to be poured somewhere Monday morning. It looked like I was going to dig these trenches myself... until I called Will. I'd only exchanged cards with him a few days prior, and I didn't expect him to agree to the job, considering the timing and the whopping ten bucks an hour paycheck. And yet from the other end of the phone, I heard an amicable, "Sure."

When he showed up the following day to help finish the job, I really didn't know what to think—I lived in the construction world of broken promises and when things went well, it was time to figure out how in the hell that happened. Neither one of us could have imagined the next trench we'd find ourselves in, desperately digging together.

By the end of the weekend, we had thoroughly enjoyed each other's company, almost like two old souls. We quickly reached that stage of two people who know one another well enough that they don't feel like they have to talk. After the end of the second sweat-soaked day, I asked Will if he would like to come to work with me and grow this homebuilding company. With an honest grin and the now-familiar enthusiasm, he said, "Yeah, sure I would."

Will and I became fast friends. We worked hard and played hard. It wasn't unusual for us to finish working early and he'd say, "Let's go rent a plane and fly over the coastline to watch the sharks that no one can see from the beach." That was about the most exciting thing you could say to me—it was through Will that I discovered my fascination and love of being up in the air. Yes, things were really good.

But in four months, that all changed. Will's pilot friend, Erik, called me with some terrible news. He told me that Will was in jail. It was a surreal conversation; I had a terrible time wrapping my head around what Erik was telling me. What in the world just happened? Little did I know the roller coaster my life was going to be the next two and a half years. More importantly, the hell my friend was going to be subjected to.

This book details that roller coaster. The horrific and brutal existence. The human spirit depleting terrors. But Will found strength in the depths of his mind, spirit, and friends that would lead him out of the hell he was in.

I had a front-row seat throughout the process. And just like showing up the second day to finish digging the ditch, Will kept showing up every day to keep his focus on crossing the finish line. What follows is my friend's journey back. Buckle up. You're in for a bumpy yet satisfying ride.

Larry Brindley

Table of Contents

Introduction ... 5
Chapter 1: **Steady Climbing** ... 7
Chapter 2: **A Day None of Us Will Forget** ... 15
Chapter 3: **Before the Storm** ... 27
Chapter 4: **Accusations and Changes** ... 33
Chapter 5: **Things Get Real** ... 40
Chapter 6: **Nothing to Do but Wait** ... 50
Chapter 7: **We Go to Trial** ... 60
Chapter 8: **The Deck is Stacked** ... 63
Chapter 9: **The Verdict** ... 76
Chapter 10: **Hell Part One** ... 85
Chapter 11: **Nash Prison-Maximum Security** ... 95
Chapter 12: **Larry's Brilliant Idea** ... 108
Chapter 13: **Back to Court-Redemption** ... 118
Chapter 14: **Emotional Meltdown** ... 124
Epilogue ... 133
Acknowledgements ... 137
About the Author ... 138

Introduction

"I'm looking for a Mr. William Smith," he said in a not-too-friendly tone.

"I'm William Smith." I replied, realizing the courtesy of a *hello* wasn't likely.

Turned out, the burly visitor was a police detective. He flashed his badge in front of my face. "Can I come in?" He asked as he looked over my shoulder.

I tried to hide the mixed feelings of surprise, nervousness, and anger that impulsively coursed through me. I forced a smile and stepped aside opening the door wide enough for him to enter. He took two taps to get the snow off each of his black dress shoes, as he entered my house. Watching the back of his head, I could tell he was scoping out my place. I didn't know what he was expecting to find but I think it disappointed him that all he found was a man who had been woken from a nap.

"What can I do for you Mr.....?" I gave him the clue to tell me his name. He didn't bite.

"You are being accused of perpetrating an alleged rape."

Captain Will Smith

For a moment I thought one of my friends must have put someone up to this and he wasn't a real cop. That must be why he just flashed his badge so quickly and hadn't identified himself.

"Excuse me?" I asked. "Come again..."

He gave me an exasperated look. "Rape, Mr. Smith. You are accused of rape."

Chapter 1

Steady Climbing

I was born in Raleigh on Sept. 10, 1973 to Mr. and Mrs. William B. and Lillian L Smith. My sister Nancy is 18 years my senior, so we only lived together at my parents' house during my first year of life, after which she left to study nursing. So for all intents and purposes, I was an only child. I could honestly say I had a happy childhood. I had the full support of both my parents, who thought the world of me, and always encouraged me to pursue my dreams. I realize now how much that helped me to strive and survive the many trials I was destined to overcome during my young adult life.

A glitch in my perfect world happened when I was seven-years old. My parents got divorced. My dad moved to Virginia Beach and I would get on a plane and visit him every other weekend.

To make ends meet my mother worked three jobs. I attended private elementary school. With less time required for study, and with my mother working so often, I had ample time to be an active participant in the school's athletic program. I would literally spend hours on any given day kicking a football.

Later, when I was about to start high school, it was decided that I needed to be with him full-time (a boy needs his dad sometimes) and moved to live with him. Since I played a lot of soccer in my youth and became quite good at it, when I got to Virginia, I easily made the soccer team and became one of their best players. Although I didn't have many friends, I managed to enjoy the transition from private to public school. Due to my advanced academics from private schooling, public school was easy for me. I also made the high school football team and easily won the role as the starting kicker. Before I left, I had set the record for the longest field goal in the school's history at the time. I spent a lot of quality time with my dad which helped me grow as a young man and gave me a road map to becoming a good father in the future. My favorite pastime with my dad had always been building electric train sets. To this day I keep a beautiful Lionel 1964 vintage set in my basement.

I didn't realize it then, but my parents' divorce and seeing my mother struggle with life as a single parent, cemented in me an insatiable drive to seize every opportunity life gave me. I learned how to avoid the pitfalls that swallow those who spend all day complaining and feeling sorry for themselves instead of picking up a shovel to dig their way out. Whether it was sports or schoolwork, I told myself over and over again that I would never give up and always give my best. One of my mom's jobs consisted of being the caretaker for a self-made millionaire named Charles Caldwell, who made his fortune selling tires. While mom took care of him and his wife, I would hang out in their mansion and sometimes helped the old man tend to his dogs. Mr. Caldwell loved dogs so much that, in his 40-acre estate, every one of his dogs had their own trailer that served as a fully equipped doghouse. These little dog-homes were complete with running water, electricity, and all the canine commodities you could imagine. I also mowed his extensive lawn to get some spending money and help my mom.

Because he didn't have any children of his own, the old man grew fond of me and I got to like him a lot as well. I used to spend hours listening to his colorful stories on how he made his fortune. Unknown to me, this experience was honing my entrepreneurial instincts and etching in my mind what would later become part of my foundation for survival and my road map to success.

Many years later, good old Caldwell passed and it turned out that he had made a deal with his business partner whereby his partner got the property to sell for development, and my mother got to keep the house. We stayed on that property for four years before I moved for high school and later I would visit her there often. When my mother finally sold it, she made so much money that for Christmas that year she bought me a five-bedroom house, a Harley, and a brand-new BMW!

I was the envy of every 18-year-old I knew. Talk about graduation presents.

After high school I attended Chowan College, a small private university in Murfreesboro, North Carolina. I enjoyed college and felt like a million bucks, driving my Beemer around campus. I also made kicker on the football team as a freshman. During my first spring break, I made a trip to Florida and just fell in love with it. The following semester I transferred to Hillsborough Community College in Tampa and moved into a nice apartment there with a buddy of mine and we began *livin' la vida loca*. I lasted at HCC for 16 months. I dropped out and opted to spend my nights partying in Ybor City instead, chasing girls and enjoying life in paradise. That's when I met Shannon, who soon became my wife.

Shannon and I got pregnant, so we decided to get married right away. To assume my responsibilities as a dad-to-be, I took a job at Chili's, where I soon became a shift manager. We celebrated our wedding at the Don Cesar Hotel in St. Pete Beach. Pastor Higgins consecrated our vows in a traditional ceremony where 200 guests, four bridesmaids, and four groomsmen witnessed our legal union. Soon after the wedding, I transferred to the Olive Garden as the restaurant manager for a while before moving back to North Carolina.

William Alexander Beach Smith was born on Nov.16, in Raleigh, North Carolina. Naturally, Shannon and I loved our first-born immensely and I thought my family was going to endure and grow together. I really wanted to give it my all as a husband and as a father. At the time, I was managing a restaurant called George's Garage, in Durham, but I was just about fed up with the entire restaurant business. My motivation was low and I needed a change. I wanted to do something else, be someone else. I needed a fresh start. I was desperate for a new and exciting way to make a better living for my family.

One morning, on my way to work, I saw an outdoor billboard showing a small airplane towing a Fly-By sign with the slogan *Discover Freedom*. I memorized the telephone number and jotted it down as soon as I arrived at the restaurant. Two weeks later I quit my job and discovered that I had very few options. I had no idea what I was going to do next, I just knew something had to change

Then I remembered the slogan - *Discover Freedom*.

The next morning, during a family meeting, I announced my decision to go into aviation. Right off the bat, my mother-in-law pulled a classic response of disapproval.

"A pilot? Only smart people can be pilots. He didn't say pilot, did he?"

"Mom!" Shannon yelled.

"What? He's not that smart." My mother-in-law looked around innocently, "Did I say something wrong?"

My mom was also hesitant, but not because she didn't think I was smart enough. She was concerned for my safety. Many people, particularly people my mother's age viewed flying as a dangerous occupation at that time.

With the lukewarm blessing from my family, I signed up for a demonstration flight the next day. It was a beautiful morning and the adrenaline rush I felt as I approached the flight school's hangar was beyond compare. My instructor was the kind of guy that exudes so much confidence in what he is doing that you would trust him with your life in any aircraft. After conducting his pre-flight checks, the pilot revved up the Lycoming 4 cylinder, horizontally opposed 160 horsepower engine that propelled the Cessna 172 to the skies for my discovery flight.

The purring of the engine filled me with a sense of anticipation. That enticing sound was accompanied by the rolling of the wheels as we taxied to the runway and, before I realized it, everything changed. I experienced the thrill and beauty of flight. Those twenty minutes in the air changed my life.

I had discovered freedom.

Because I didn't have the $6,000 needed to complete my flight school and get my pilot's license, I started working at H&H Propeller, overhauling engines and other aircraft components while studying to get my private pilot's license. It was a win-win situation, because everyone at the shop was either certified or knew just about everything related to my newfound passion. I delved eagerly into all aspects of flight and breezed through both the practical and the theoretical certification exams.

I continued to pursue my professional career in aviation by enrolling in ComAir Aviation Academy in Sanford, Florida. I took their accelerated course and did two years of training in eight months. There I received my Instrument, Commercial, and Flight Instructor's certificate. It's the equivalent of a commercial driver's license so that a pilot can get paid for his services. My $72,000 investment would finally start paying off. I could now start making money.

As soon as I got my diploma, I applied for a job as a flight instructor and was readily hired. That's where I first met Jill, who was one of my first flight students. I actually never finished teaching the course though, because midway through the program I received a phone call from Colgan Airways, which is US Airways express. They wanted to interview me for a pilot's position and offered to fly me to Manassas, Virginia. However, I felt it would make a better impression if I flew myself there and was given permission from the flight school to take one of their planes. During the interview, a chief pilot said I was the first job applicant he had known that had flown himself to an interview. They offered me the job and I was beyond ecstatic. My dreams were about to come true. I had just landed my first 121 job, which is sort of an apprenticeship for pilots for a commercial carrier. I happily transferred Jill and the rest of my small group of students to a different instructor so I could begin a flying career. I was going to be a legitimate pilot!

However, while my professional life was literally taking off, my constant traveling as well as other issues were beginning to take a toll on my relationship with Shannon. We knew we were growing apart, but we didn't know how to change course. We hardly saw each other because I was traveling most of the time, and because of that we were living in different cities. Eventually, it got to the point where Shannon began feeling very lonely and depressed. It got so bad that she filed for divorce during the summer of 2001.

My separation and subsequent divorce from Shannon marked a new chapter in my life. I was enjoying my new career and really thought I was going to make it big in the airline business. I was either going to start my own flight school, go into crop dusting, fly commercial planes for a major airline, or who knows, maybe even start my own commuter airline years down the line. No law-abiding citizen pictures their future behind bars, fighting for their freedom. I sure didn't. Whatever scenario I played out in my mind, I always imagined myself happy and successful.

But I was wrong. Dead wrong.

Chapter 2

A Day None of us Will Forget

Weeks later I was occupying one of the many empty tables at an IHOP near Logan Airport in Boston when I saw an American Airlines pilot walk in. He was tall and slender with salt and pepper hair. According to his uniform and rank, he was a senior officer. He spotted me too, and gave me a head nod. I motioned to him to come over. Even though I was still a rookie pilot, I already knew that pilots got lonely, particularly when "dead heading," - airline-speak for being en route from one airport to another.

"Are you doing a solo meal?" he asked in pilot jargon. His voice sounded as if he could do radio.

"Not anymore," I answered. "Please sit down."

I introduced myself and we exchanged credentials and other basic information that members of the airline industry usually share when getting acquainted. He was at the end of a 30-year career and was now flying a Boeing 757 for American Airlines. In the piloting business, you get to fly bigger and more sophisticated aircraft the longer you stay active.

"I've had my share of flights, including jumps over the pond (meaning flying over the ocean)," he said. "I'm only flying in the states until retirement. After having logged thousands of hours of flight time, he had reached the status that allowed him to choose his routes and, although he didn't tell me, I knew he was making very good money.

He told me he had a wife and two kids who were both in college. "I'm taking a month's vacation after these next flights. Getting ready to spend some quality time with my family," he said.

"I hear ya," I told him. You don't get much of that with this career. Cost me my marriage. I miss spending time with my kids."

"Sounds like you have AIDS" he said laughing

"What?"

"Airline Induced Divorce Syndrome. I've managed to avoid it but it wasn't easy. My wife may be a saint." He answered with a hearty chuckle.

I laughed so hard I nearly cried. *What a great guy*, I thought. *This is a real role model.*

So there I was, the night of my 27th birthday on Sept. 10, 2001, a rookie pilot comparing notes with a senior honcho who was just doing easy jumps at the end of his career. As I ate my steak and eggs, I told him how inspiring it was to listen to his anecdotes and that I knew

I could learn from his wealth of experiences. This fueled his curiosity to ask questions about my training, and in a genuine gesture of camaraderie, he offered some good advice. After conversing for nearly an hour, he was ready to order coffee, and since I don't drink coffee at night and had finished eating, we shook hands and parted ways. I figured I'd bump into him again sometime soon since we were staying at the same hotel. As I was about to leave the restaurant, I looked back to waive goodbye to my new friend, the person who I wanted to be like in thirty years. He raised his coffee mug in a friendly salute. I could not have known that I would be one of the last people to see him alive.

The next morning I sluggishly woke up to my alarm at 7 a.m. to go to Logan. After breakfast I took the shuttle van from the hotel to the airport with crew members from other airlines. We heard on the radio an initial report that a small aircraft had slammed into a building in Manhattan. I thought, *Some dumbass in a Cessna 172 flew himself into a tower.*

As we were leaving the van the radio report said it was a larger, twin-engine commuter plane. *It must have been foggy with low visibility*, I reasoned. I didn't think too much about it then, since I was busy going through security and getting my clearance to proceed to the crew quarters below the main floor next to the luggage area.

I found my captain in an area under the terminal that housed a huge pilots' lounge. He told me to go to the airplane we were about to fly and conduct the pre-flight checks. I jokingly asked if he had heard about the

Captain Will Smith

dumb fuck that had flown into the side of a building. We both laughed and I went to conduct my pre-flight, first inside the airplane, starting at the cockpit, checking all instruments, and then walking to visually inspect the passenger area.

As I was checking the exterior of the airplane, including wingtips, tires, engines, and the overall condition of the fuselage, I was approached by a man in a gray jacket wearing sunglasses with credentials around his neck identifying him as an officer from the Federal Aviation Administration.

"Sir, please follow me into the terminal. I need to ask you some questions," he said. He was a clean-shaven older man who sounded as if he had smoked too many cigarettes.

"Can it wait? I need to finish up my pre-flight." I replied.

"No, it can't. Besides, there won't be any flights arriving or departing for the rest of the day." I began to walk with him towards the terminal. I was about to ask him what was going on but, at that point, another agent, who later introduced himself as being from the FBI, approached us.

"What is your business with this plane?" he demanded, pointing at the plane I had been inspecting. Because he used the word plane and not aircraft, I assumed the he wasn't part of the FAA.

"What? I'm doing my job. What's going on?"

"What job?" he asked, still with an edge to his voice.

"I'm a pilot." I pointed to the badge on my uniform. "I was doing the pre-flight inspection on this aircraft. We are repositioning this particular aircraft to Manassas later today."

"Son, you aren't going anywhere today. Haven't you heard what's going on?" the FAA agent asked.

I looked at them with a blank expression. Before I could ask a question, the FBI agent spoke.

"We are under attack," he said, his voice simmering with rage.

I looked around, not noticing anything out of the ordinary in my immediate surroundings. "What are you talking about? Under attack from who?" I stopped walking and after another step, they stopped and turned to me.

"Did you hear about the plane that struck one of the Twin Towers?" the FBI agent asked.

"I heard that some dumbass flew into the side of a building, but I didn't know it was one of the Twin Towers."

The men glanced at each other. Then the FBI agent looked hard at me for a few seconds. It appeared that if I was under some sort of suspicion, I had somehow absolved myself. In a softer tone, he spoke, "That plane was a 757. It was hijacked out of this airport." I couldn't believe what he was saying. "The hijackers that took over that plane came in on the plane you were inspecting right now." I froze like a deer staring at headlights.

"You have to be fucking kidding me, right?" That was the only way I thought to respond.

As we continued walking back to the terminal, he explained that the aircraft was being confiscated to remove the last four rows of seats for DNA testing to identify the perpetrators. I was escorted to the passenger area because the crewmembers' area had been evacuated. As I approached, I saw my friend Jody, surrounded by other pilots, American Airlines executives, and what I assumed were other federal agents. I could see she was distressed, so I went to her to see what other news I could find out.

"I should have done something," she said in between soft sobs. "It was cold outside, yet they were sweating. I should have noticed. I could have stopped this." I instantly realized that she was the pilot that flew the aircraft from Maine that brought in the hijackers. I placed my arm around her and tried to console her out of her self-imposed guilt. I told her that it wasn't her fault and that she shouldn't blame herself.

Then, just as my captain walked in, someone in the room gasped loudly. I looked up at one of the television monitors and saw a second aircraft hit the south tower. The deadliest silence I can remember permeated through the entire room in what seemed like a suspension of time. And then, the sounds of uncontrollable weeping and sobbing, blended with oaths of rage and despair, filled the air as men, women, and children wallowed in the horror that shook the nation.

After the initial shock of what had happened faded, the patriotic warrior in me swelled up with anger at what had been perpetrated on our soil. I felt violated by this cowardly attack on our freedom and our way of life. I really felt like strapping myself to the cockpit of an F16 and going to kick some ass. My heart was jumping inside my chest as I shared this anger with others around me. I wasn't the only one, either. Deep outrage or painful sorrow had overtaken everyone in the terminal. Those same emotions reverberated across the country.

I wanted to get to a phone and talk to my family to let them know I was not on board one of those planes. They knew I was in Boston, but didn't know which flights I would be facilitating. However, all cell phone communication was dead. There was no way for me to communicate to anyone outside of the terminal. It seemed as if the world had come to a standstill.

Time passed slowly, but eventually I found myself at a Starbucks in the terminal. There, I saw the attack on the Pentagon on another monitor. That was the last thing I needed to see for the full scope of this concerted terrorist attack on the United States of America to sink in. My mind began to wander into different possible scenarios. Mass mobilization of troops; the president on board Air Force One communicating with the Joint Chiefs of Staff; the War Room buzzing with orders to deploy all land, sea, and air capabilities against the perpetrators. This had to mean war. America is going to war! This, I thought, might very well be the beginning of WW III.

I walked past a group of pilots huddled in front of a TV. They were trying to make some sense of what their eyes were seeing. I saw mothers holding their children and crying with them. A few feet away from me a woman was half pleading and half screaming at her husband, looking for answers. What she was really looking for, what everyone sought, was hope. There was a convoluted sense of fear, desperation, sadness, anger, and rage in everybody's voice.

"Are we next?"

"Who could possibly do this to us?"

"How could this happen?"

"Does anyone know anyone in those planes?"

"Officer, are we safe?" This question was asked directly to me. I looked at the three women who had approached me. One of them was holding a sleeping little girl and another a slightly bigger girl's hand. "Is there an evacuation plan? Who is protecting us?"

As I searched for the right way to ease their fears, another woman approached, with dried tears streaking her face. "I'm from New York," she said. Everyone in our vicinity got quiet. "I'm on my way to LaGuardia. When can I get on my connecting flight?" I thought she was going to fall prey to hysteria, but she took a deep breath, and although visibly shaken, she remained calm.

There I was, trying to get word out to my family that I was safe, that I wasn't on that plane, but in front of me was a woman whose family lived in New York. She desperately wanted to know if they were okay. Just then an announcement was made over the terminal intercom system, "Everyone please remain calm. No one is allowed to go outside until further notice. We will make more announcements as the situation unfolds. Please remain calm. Thank you for your cooperation."

"I'm so sorry," I said to the small group who looked to me for answers. "I only know as much as you do." I looked at the girl who held her mother's hand. "But I'm sure we are going to be okay," I said with a forced smile. "Nobody does this to us and gets away with it."

* * * *

Throughout the rest of the day, as the pieces of the attack began to come together, I realized that these were no ordinary mercenaries, but well-trained and skillful operatives following a carefully designed master plan. They came in from Canada to the U.S. through Rockland, Maine, through a small airport with a trailer for a terminal, which had no sophisticated electronic detection devices. It was quite easy for the terrorists to smuggle their lethal knife cutters.

As I was pondering this, the news unfolded. President George W. Bush, who had spent the day being shuttled around the country because of security concerns, returned to the White House. At 9 p.m. he delivered a televised address from the Oval Office, declaring, "Terrorist attacks can shake the foundations of our biggest buildings, but they cannot touch the foundation of America. These acts shatter steel, but they cannot

I was hoping against hope that I would keep my job, but the pilots that were safe were the ones that had built up tenure over the years. Stark reality hit me in the face. America was going to war and I had just lost my livelihood. The hole I felt in the middle of my chest was as heavy as an elephant's leg. I sat there in silence for a moment. Then I lost it. I let out all the emotions as I realized the magnitude of the terrorist attacks not only on the country but on my life. I didn't know how I was going to provide for my sons. I cried with my head down and tears flooded over the sunglasses I wore.

"Is everything all right?" I looked up to see a concerned flight attendant. There were a lot of people crying those days, so seeing me cry must not have been a major shock to her. "Are you okay? Can I get you a drink?"

I took a couple of deep breaths, forcing myself to get a hold on my emotions. "Yes, I'm sure everything will work out all right. Please, get me a Jack and Coke." As she turned to leave I added, "Make it a double."

Falling From The Sky

I arrived, unannounced, one evening from training and found a rather large group of people partying at my house. Ordinarily I would have just eased into the party and let my hair down, except for the fact that there were some shady characters there. Jill had invited known drug dealers, even though I had previously told her that I didn't want them in my house. So instead of jumping into the party, I shut it down. When Jill noticed that people were leaving, she became incensed.

"What the fuck, Will?" I could tell she was coked up.

"You know I don't want those guys here!" I yelled. "Why did you invite them?"

"They're my friends. You can't just come here, kick my friends out, and embarrass me like that."

I felt like I was talking to a teenage girl who was throwing a tantrum because she couldn't get her way. "I can kick anyone out of my house that I want to," I answered. "Anyone!" That was my way of giving her a hint to watch how she talked to me or I would kick her out next. But I don't know if it was the cocaine, the booze, or the embarrassment that fueled her because she got even more confrontational with me.

"That's bullshit. This is my house, too. I live here, too."

I couldn't believe that she felt as if she, a guest who didn't pay rent or for food, had the same rights to my house as I did. The few remaining people there were silent and just watched us go back and forth for a while longer. I couldn't reason with her; she was in another state of mind entirely. Our argument got worse and insults flew back and forth until I realized what I had to do.

"Jill, this isn't going to work out. You have to leave," I said calmly, with my hands on my hips.

"I'm not leaving," was her response. "You know I don't have anywhere to go. Don't be an asshole."

We argued about that for a while until I went up to the room I was letting her sleep in and grabbed an armful of clothes and threw them out on my front yard. Instead of trying to reason with me, she became even more belligerent. Without remorse, I kicked her out of my house that night. I'm not sure where she went, but I heard she wound up in Champagne, Illinois.

* * * *

Time went on, and on Andrew's birthday, my friends and I went bar hopping to celebrate. . Carlton said to me, "Guess who's back around?"

"Who?"

"Your buddy Jill," he said with a smile. They had imitated and acted out our fight more times than a Seinfeld rerun. I don't know if he thought I was going to disparage her, but I just shrugged my shoulders. "If it's okay with you, I asked her to come out with us tonight."

I laughed. "It's funny that first you ask her to come out with us and then ask me if it's okay."

"Well . . . is it?" he asked.

"Sure, I don't care."

And I didn't. She and I had gotten in that public argument, but prior to that one time, we had always gotten along. Besides, she was fun to party with. We continued to enjoy the evening and a lot of people wound up at my house, the crash pad, when the bars shut down. We continued to party for a while longer until most people either fell asleep or left. Andrew and his girlfriend went to a room and then Carlton and his girlfriend took another room shortly thereafter. Later that night, I was in my kitchen eating a sandwich when Jill burst into my house, hoping to see the party still rolling.

"Hey, Will," she said sweetly.

I smiled back. "Hey, Jill."

Then she looked around and her smile slowly faded. "Where is everybody? I thought we were partying?"

I told her that Carlton and Andrew were in two of the bedrooms with their girlfriends and everyone else was partied out for the night. I could tell that she was disappointed.

"Is it okay if I go upstairs for a bit?" she asked. I gestured with the sandwich in my left hand that it was fine with me and she turned and went up the stairs. In a little while, I finished my sandwich and went upstairs. When I opened the door to my room, there she was on her knees in my bed . . . topless.

"Really?" I asked. She wagged her finger motioning for me to come in. We had both been drinking, but knew exactly what we were doing. One thing led to another, we got naked, had sex, and fell asleep.

* * * *

The next morning I woke up to Jill sleeping peacefully next to me. I got out of bed, careful not to wake her, slipped into my robe and went downstairs for some coffee. I was accustomed to the shambles a night of partying did to my house and I expertly sidestepped over shoes and people on the way to my kitchen.

I found my buddy John in the kitchen finishing his last sip of coffee. After a brief exchange, he went upstairs. Shortly thereafter, coffee in hand, I went to my bedroom, but the door was locked. I figured John was in there and had woken Jill up. I didn't know what they were doing and I didn't care, so I went downstairs to finish my java.

A little while later Jill came running down the stairs, swearing like a sailor while trying to put on her left shoe.

"What's going on?" I asked.

"My boyfriend is blowing up my phone, my mother is texting me to find out where I am, and I think I'm going to miss my fuckin' flight!"

Classic Jill. I wished her well and she hurriedly got in her car and drove away. Shortly thereafter my friend John came downstairs and promptly left without a goodbye. I never saw or heard from him again.

Ever.

Chapter 4

Accusations and Changes

If it's true that we all learn from our mistakes, at least most of the time, it's also true that sometimes we ignore signs of trouble when they pop up in our lives. Such was the case for me when, on one cold November morning in 2001 while spending quality time with my kids over the Thanksgiving weekend, I got a call from Jill out of the blue.

"This is a surprise," I said. "How've you been? I haven't heard from you in a while."

"Yeah, well, you know why," she answered. I had no idea what she was talking about, but I figured that since her parents and boyfriend were looking for her on the last night she stayed at my house, she had gotten in some kind of trouble with them and wanted to steer clear from my friends and me. Or maybe she felt weird that we had sex after being friends for so long.

"I guess," I said, not being sure how else to respond.

Then she totally threw me off. "It wasn't right of you to take advantage of me the way you did." Our short conversation went from mildly uncomfortable to absurd.

"What are you talking about?" I got up and left the room so that my sons couldn't hear my side of the conversation.

"I was so drunk that night and you totally did whatever you wanted to me without me even realizing what was going on."

"What did you just say? Could you repeat that?" I was trying to be cool but was having trouble trying to hide my anger at this point.

"Will, you know I didn't want to have sex with you, but you took advantage of me because I was drunk." We got quiet for a moment. Then she said it. "You fucking raped me, Will," she exclaimed with a passion that froze my blood.

"What the fuck are you talking about? I went to my bedroom and you were on my bed topless. How did I take advantage of you?" We started going back and forth and I felt like I was arguing with the Jill that I couldn't reason with again. If anything it was her who practically raped me!

I had no idea that our conversation was being taped. Someone had put her up to this and all they wanted was for me to admit having sex with her. It didn't matter that I admitted to having consensual sex with her. I guess they believed that they could work around that. Once I agreed that we did have sex, she got off the phone and left me bewildered, hundreds of miles away.

Suddenly my older son William interrupted my thoughts with news that his baby brother Giff had just swallowed a piece of wire, like a safety pin or something. I dropped the phone and ran as fast as I could up the stairs only to find Giff curiously playing with a wire clothes hanger.

"Will, is that what you were yelling about?" I asked.

He gave me that innocent smile that he knew turned me completely harmless. It's alarming how fast kids learn to become master manipulators. I went about giving Giff a thorough oral exam, just in case. I realized that what my sons really needed was uninterrupted time with their daddy. I gestured to my firstborn, and holding Giff in my arms, little Will followed me to the basement to carry on a family tradition handed down from my dad to me - playing with the electric train set.

After some great train-time with my boys, the phone rang again and I thought: "Oh no, not Jill again!" I went up the stairs to where I had left the cell phone and when I picked it up, to my relief the name on the screen read "Shannon."

"What's up, Shannon?" I answered with an upbeat tone.

"Boy, you're in a good mood today; what's the occasion?" she replied.

"I'm just having a great time with the kids. We're going to the mall today to have lunch and then we're going to watch a movie," I explained, retaining my jovial mood.

"Sounds great!"

Yet, knowing her as I do, I sensed tension in her voice. I thought maybe it had to do with our divorce or something with the kids. "Everything ok?" I asked.

"I don't mean to ruin your mood, but I need someone to talk to."

"You got me here," I said. "What's wrong?"

"Dad's not feeling well. I'm very worried," she said, almost sobbing. "I'm afraid of losing him. I think he's going to die on us soon. But don't tell the kids please, I want them to enjoy their time with you and not to worry. They know he's sick, but they don't know how sick."

I agreed, and after we hung up I got the somber feeling that my father-in-law was not going to be around much longer. Three days later, Shannon called to inform me her dad had passed away.

"I'm sorry, Shannon; I really am. You know how much I loved your father, honey," I said. "I'll get down there tonight to be with you, your mother, and the kids."

I could hear her sobbing quietly on the other end, like a little girl lost in a shopping mall. During the long silence that ensued, I thought of the old man and all he had done to try to help us through. He was an old warrior who never quit believing in me and was always telling his daughter how he valued my friendship and how he thought I was the best man she was ever going to get. I really liked Don a lot, and I was already missing him dearly. When we hung up the phone I began to mourn him.

Ronald Gilford was a prominent attorney in the Tampa community. Well over 1,000 people attended his funeral. After the funeral, I returned to my home alone and with a deep empty feeling. It was an awkward sense of loss because the bonds that had tied me to Ron and his family were fading, not only due to his death, but because my life with his daughter was coming to a close. My mind was lost on what I had with Shannon and how I thought my life would have been had we stayed together.

You lose track of where love and affection ends and when indifference unwittingly takes over. You wish it would never start, but once it does, you just desperately want the transition to come to an end. It's tough when something that was once your reason for living dies inside of you. I understood the full weight and gravity what the consequences of divorce were having on my heart. Ron's loss hit me harder than I thought it would, because not only did I miss Ron, but I also missed the family unit I once had more than ever. I turned on the radio to try to escape, but there was no escaping the ache in my heart. I was in training and couldn't leave to be there with Shannon and the boys. I had to go through the pain all alone.

A few weeks later, Shannon called me again.

"Will, we have to talk." I knew what that meant when she said that. I braced myself to receive bad news.

"What is it, Shannon?" I replied politely and genuinely concerned. "Are the kids and your mother all right? How are you guys holding up? What can I do for you?"

"Mom has decided we are not going to celebrate Christmas this year. We are all still too depressed by dad's passing. Neither of us are in the mood for decorating or shopping. We just don't have the energy for all that," she explained.

"Nonsense," I replied. "You know how much the season means to the kids. This is Christmas we're talking about. If anything, it's imperative for the boys that Santa shows up this year."

I didn't want to start an argument with Shannon over this, so I just told her I was going to come over to spend Christmas with the kids, to which she reluctantly agreed. We let it go at that and not another word was spoken on the issue. On the afternoon of Dec. 23 Santa Will appeared at the Gilford's driveway in a big black sleigh, my Ford Excursion.

"Daddy, Daddy!" little Will yelled as he spotted my truck pulling up. The SUV was filled to the brim with Christmas presents for the kids, Shannon, and her mother. It also carried a Christmas tree, lights, decorations, and everything else necessary to light up the Christmas spirit. The spirit of Christmas invaded their once gloomy house and they all joined in to set up the tree and decorate the living room. The sadness of death disappeared.

We all had a great Christmas. Little did I know it would be the last Christmas we would spend together as a family. I never knew how much my life was going to change in January of the following year, just a week away.

Chapter 5

Things Get Real

It was a cool, sunny morning in the outskirts of Raleigh, North Carolina. There was still snow on the ground as a reminder of the vicious storm that had swept through the area a few days before. The early morning chill was accentuated by the gentle but steady howling of that windy winter day. Our driveway was iced over, which meant I was going to encounter slippery driving conditions when I drove out for groceries later.

The mere thought of grabbing the cold steering wheel made me shiver, so I cuddled up underneath my warm quilt and attempted to go back to sleep. Just then I heard the crunching sound of approaching tires over the ice and, as I peeked out the window, a black Crown Victoria slowed to a stop in my driveway. At first I thought, *oh no, another salesman.* What a crappy way to make a living in the middle of the winter. But when a tall, overweight, and rough-looking man got out of the car, I had the impression that he was here on some other business.

As I pulled my robe on, my doorbell rang twice, one right after the other. I walked down the stairs a little more quickly than I normally would have, figuring that the poor guy was freezing outside. As I opened the door, my thought was to politely dismiss this intruder who was disrupting my sleep as quickly as possible and get back under the enticing warmth of my comforter.

"I'm looking for a Mr. William Smith," the burly visitor said in a not-too-friendly tone.

I look back on that one moment in time and wonder if, perhaps I hadn't opened the door that morning, if all of this would have equated to a bad dream. But I did open the door, let trouble in, and after a short, unpleasant exchange, heard the words that I still hear in my nightmares, the words that forever changed my life.

"You are being accused of perpetrating an alleged rape."

"Excuse me?" I asked. "Come again . . . ?"

He gave me an exasperated look. "Rape, Mr. Smith. You are accused of rape."

My heart was in my throat as I realized that this man was indeed a police officer and he was serious. My mind quickly scrolled through the women I had known since I had separated from my wife. I'd had my share of girlfriends and flings but no one came to mind that actually hated me enough to accuse me of rape. And then, in an instant, I remembered my exchange with Jill.

"Rape? Are you sure you have the right Will Smith?" I asked.

"Do you know a girl named Jill? She reportedly stayed here with you a few months ago," he said flatly.

" Oh, Boy!" I said with a sarcastic laugh. "Yeah, I know Jill\She's a former flight student of mine who I made the mistake of allowing to stay at my house for a short while. She was a stripper at the time and quite a party girl. We had a falling out and I asked her to leave but we reconnected months later and left on good terms. If she's saying I raped her, you might want to look into her background," My tone was quite sardonic and he responded angrily.

Mistaking my nerves for disrespect he answered,. "There is nothing funny about rape, Mr. Smith," his teeth clenched. He reminded me of Agent Smith from the Matrix movies, same bad tie, same bad attitude, and no sense of humor.

"No, you don't understand because you don't know Jill. She . . ."

"She is accusing you of rape and I find your attitude to be contemptuous and in bad character. I'm here for your statement," he said as he looked for a place to sit down.

"Statement?" I echoed. My casual dismal of all this quickly disappeared as I realized for the first time, without a doubt, that there was a police officer in my house, wanting my statement about an alleged rape. I couldn't believe this was actually happening.

"What happened on the night of . . ."

"I'm calling my lawyer," I said, interrupting him. He stepped close to me in an aggressive manner. Instinctively I put a hand up between us.

"You are not calling a lawyer!" he shouted. "I am here for your statement and then I'm leaving. If you are as innocent as you're claim to be, there is no reason for you not to give me a statement."

I was at a loss of what to do. Would I really look guilty if I called a lawyer? Mr. No-name cop got quite upset at me for even suggesting one. However, I trusted him less than he trusted lawyers.

"I'm not going to be bullied by you. I am getting a lawyer," I said as I turned towards the door to let him out. "If you'll be so kind, please leave now." I realized, though, that he hadn't followed me.

"I'm not leaving here without my statement." His eyes burned through me as if I had personally done something to him. "Lawyers just complicate things and you don't want this to get complicated, believe me when I tell you." He scanned the room again, his face barely masking disgust. "You are already in a lot of trouble; don't make it worse for yourself."

I couldn't believe he was trying this hard to intimidate me. I'd been awake for less than fifteen minutes and this conversation was going way too fast for me. "It's my right to get a lawyer and I will not let you dictate how I'm going to handle this ridiculous accusation. Please leave."

"Listen to me carefully, Mr. Smith." he said, pulling out a notebook and a pen. He pointed the pen at my face, "If you get a lawyer, I guarantee you that I'll make sure they put you in prison."

In response to his threat I reached out and opened the door but he didn't budge.

"I'll leave when I'm good and ready. You are in a lot of trouble, mister, and I am not leaving without my statement."

That was how I found out I was actually being accused of raping Jill. The same party girl that had slept with several of my friends and co-workers at pilot training school. Jill, who crawled naked into my bed and pulled me down to her to have sex with her. *What kind of sick game is she playing here,* I thought. *What does she want? Money? Revenge for kicking her out.* I had no clue, but I damn well planned to find out.

The detective looked at me in disgust, and it began to sink in that this was as serious a matter as I had ever had to deal with. He asked me several more times for my statement before he realized that he couldn't coerce me to speak without my lawyer present.

With a terse comment and shrewd look, he passed by me as I kept the door open for him to leave. The cold wind that bit into me served as a reminder that I wasn't dreaming. Right before I was about to shut the door I saw the detective wobble a little but then regain his footing. However, his next step betrayed him and he fell hard on his back on my icy driveway. For a moment

I forgot the predicament I was in and let out a laugh. A laugh that he heard. If he was ever going to be impartial in this matter, that reaction killed that.

Going on Empty

By the time I shut the door my mind and my heart were racing. Why would Jill say that I raped her? What will my children say? What will happen to my career as a pilot? How could this happen to me?

"Oh, my God!" I said out loud. I stared for what seemed like hours at the fireplace and I couldn't contain the feeling of despair and agony at the injustice of being accused of rape.

I would never rape a woman; that's not who I am. I'm no saint, but I was brought up with certain parameters of decency and respect that don't allow for such a thing. For me a rape is and always will be an atrocity, a violation of a person's basic dignity and self-worth.

As I began to realize the seriousness of the situation, I had to control my impulses to contact Jill and chew her out. If she was serious about all this, that would probably be construed as harassment and make matters worse. It took a concerted effort to retain my sanity and keep my fingers from dialing Jill's number. As I glared at the burnt embers in the fire pit, I couldn't help but feel that the stigma of the charges being pressed against me were threatening to burn my life into ashes of worthlessness. My chest was just about to implode from the anguish. I slowly reached for my phone and called the one person who had always and would always love me unconditionally.

"Hi mom, it's me. Listen, I have something very important to tell you," I said as a warm sense of relief invaded my being. Just hearing her voice, knowing that she was there, made me feel better.

"What is it, honey? Are you sick? What happened?" she asked, alarmed.

"Mom, it's worse than that; it's the worst thing that has ever happened to me," I said in a broken voice.

"What's going on?" she asked.

I had to tell someone and she was the only person I could confide in at this point but suddenly shame enveloped me. I shrugged my shoulders and opened my mouth to talk, but I couldn't get the words out. How could I tell my mother that I could be accused of raping a woman? Then it hit me for real that everyone I knew would find out about it. If a hole would have opened up in front of me, I would have jumped in and let the earth swallow me.

"Tell me, William!" she demanded.

"A detective just left my house."

"A detective?"

"Mom, Jill said that I raped her and he came to ask some questions." The words came out as if someone else said them. I don't know if my mother expected me to explain but I didn't know what else to say, so we said nothing while we both tried to process the implications of what I had just told her.

"But . . . but that's impossible; that's not true... is it son?"

"Of course not, mother. But if this bullshit materializes to a formal charge, I won't know what to do."

Then we began to frantically exchange information. We interrupted one another a lot as we set the course of action I needed to take. We both had a plethora of questions to which I didn't have answers. We sought the reasoning behind it all, discussed the ramifications of the charge, and discussed the barrage of emotions that this accusation stirred up in our hearts and minds.

After exhausting every detail we could think of, our conversation ended with my mom saying, "Don't worry son; you'll beat it. You're innocent. I'll be leaving here shortly and I'll be with you later today."

"Thanks, mom," I said huskily. I felt as if somehow, the cavalry was coming. I didn't know what my mother could do. I just knew that I felt better because she was going to be by my side.

A few minutes later Andrew came out of his room and I told him what had happened.

"You've got to be fucking kidding me!" he yelled. I couldn't hide the hurt, shame, embarrassment, and anger I felt. He saw it all and we sat in silence for about a minute.

"Bro. Jill?"

I nodded.

"But we all fucked her."

I nodded.

"Didn't she come over late at night and get undressed in your bed before you even got to your room?"

I nodded.

"Did you tell the cop that?"

I nodded.

It was the most one-sided conversation I had ever had. There was a river of rage welling up inside, but I didn't have an outlet for it. I wanted to punch a wall and curl up and cry like a baby at the same time. I was scared to open my mouth because I didn't know if my voice would crack from emotion.

When your world gets turned upside down like that, it's interesting the things you remember. For example, I remember staring at my quilt, wondering how it was made. Probably because I didn't want to think of anything else, but also because I was psychologically wondering what type of blankets they gave you in prison. I remember my mother coming over and cooking one of the dishes I loved, but I don't remember what it was or the taste of it. It was as if I was having an outer body experience and I couldn't connect to myself to feel, taste, smell, or even react to my surroundings. I didn't cry myself to sleep that night; I was too numb. I'm not sure that I even slept.

Hunting for Counsel

Early the following Monday morning, I mustered enough courage to make a few calls hunting for an attorney. As devastated as I was, I regained my strength by focusing on the one truth that would become the central driving force and motto of my existence - "*I am innocent!*" By day's end, I had mustered an impressive roster of potential lawyers for my case. After narrowing down the candidates to three choices, I slept on it, and by Tuesday morning I had made up my mind.

"Hello, is this the law office of Mr. George Hughes?" I asked politely.

"Yes it is, how can I help you?" a sweet female voice asked in a marked southern drawl.

"I'm William Smith. I have been referred to Mr. Hughes by an acquaintance." The well-trained legal assistant then asked me a few qualifying questions. After a brief hold, she scheduled me for a meeting in Mr. Hughes' office that Thursday at 10 a.m.

George Hughes was a prominent attorney from Raleigh. We met that Thursday for about an hour. I must have impressed him as a man who was telling the truth and who was being framed for a crime that, I not only didn't commit, but was very much opposed to. After hearing my story and holding our initial meeting, George Hughes agreed to represent me for a retainer fee of $15,000. I had a lawyer. Now we could start working on my case to prove my innocence and get over this nightmare. However, I was about to learn that some dreams, especially those really scary ones, aren't that easy to get over.

Chapter 6

Nothing to Do But Wait

I continued living as best I could under the circumstances and tried not to let this constant thorn keep me from having a positive attitude. I had been rehired by the airline. My career was back on track and everything was going well with my children. Then the inevitable happened. One brisk March morning, while I was taking a break and smoking a cigarette at Hartford's Bradley Airport, my attorney called.

"Will, you have been indicted," George said. "How soon can you show up for processing?"

"George, I'm at the middle of a four-day trip. I'll be there in a couple of days," I said.

"All right, Will. I'll call to let them know, but you have to be here no later than Wednesday."

I was very stressed out by the news, and spent the remaining days in a haze of confusion, frustration, anger, and sadness. I had to make a concerted effort to focus on my job, because flying an airplane allows little or no tolerance for making any mistakes.

Working on my case turned out to be a long and emotionally draining process. I was immersed in the quest of doing everything in my power to prove my innocence. In doing so, I realized the detective assigned to my case was not the least interested in interviewing any of my witnesses. I should have figured this from his nasty attitude during our first encounter at my home in January. He had made no effort to hide his negative attitude toward me, including threatening to put a warrant out for me. His bias against me truly materialized, though, when he neglected to interview any of my witnesses. His unfair work in acquiring all of the facts forced me to hire a private investigator to interview my witnesses to provide the evidence needed in my defense.

It was a cold morning when I went with George to the police department to turn myself in. We posted 10 percent of the $250,000 bond. My mother had to put up her house as collateral with a lien that would be removed once I appeared in court. It's funny how these things tend to have a double effect on our psyche. On one side I was grateful to mom for bailing me out, but on the other side I was crushed by the guilt of having to put my mother through this unjustified burden.

"Mom, I'm sorry for all this and how it's happening," I told her.

"That's all right, Billy," she said, using the name she had called me with since I was a little boy. "I know you're innocent," she said calmly. "The truth will come out sooner or later." We embraced in the most reassuring gesture of love. It was exactly what I needed to help me through this ordeal. I couldn't ask for a better mother than the one I have.

I was escorted down an endless maze of dark and humid corridors that led to the various processing stations. The police station was an old stone building, cold and uncomfortable. The hallways, that felt more like tunnels, had the faint odor of what I guess a dungeon would smell like. Being "processed" is a degrading ordeal. I was fingerprinted, photographed, stripped naked, and made to feel as if I was worthless.

"Have you ever felt like killing yourself, Mr. Smith?" a nasty looking overweight woman cop asked with a trace of a grin on her face. I felt like telling her that if I had to spend one day with her I would.

"No, never," I said curtly.

After the five humiliating hours of the booking process ended I was released on my own recognizance because I had paid the bail to avoid getting sent directly to the slammer. As I left the courthouse late that afternoon, I felt some relief, but I knew I was in for a fight, one that would potentially leave casualties in every area of my life.

I decided that it would be better for me to request an immediate leave of absence from my job for personal reasons instead of letting them know what I was accused of. The less they knew, the better. I made the phone call and sidestepped several questions. By the time I hung up the phone I didn't have a job. I know I still had to earn an income, though, as my legal bills were about to pile up.

A few days later, my friend Chong Dam was at my house in Westchase when a man who Chong introduced to me as Larry came to pick something up from him. During a brief introduction, Larry told me that he had started a construction company. About a week later, I called him up.

"Hey Larry, this is Will Smith. I'm Chong's friend," I said.

"Oh yeah, I remember you Will," he replied, "What's up?"

"I remember you saying that you have a construction company and I just wanted to let you know that if you ever need an extra pair of hands, I'm available."

"Well let me think for a sec," he said and paused a moment. I remained quiet, hoping he was trying to fit me in somewhere. "I could use some help digging a foundation. If you want some work, grab a shovel and meet me in the morning."

"I can do that," I said.

The next day, before I knew it, I was knee deep in a hole that I had dug. I worked side by side with Larry and another helper. We dug ditches the entire day, 50 feet long, 18 inches wide and two feet deep. When we were done, Larry asked us both to come back. On my drive home I didn't know exactly how to feel. I had been a well-respected pilot, a man who other adults called sir, but life had forced me to trade that all in to dig holes. I set my alarm to wake up the following day but I wasn't sure if I would. My arms were sore and I had gotten my clothes dirtier than ever before. The manual work was good for me though as it gave me something to do that was so physically draining that it helped me sleep all night instead of staying up wracked with anxiety.

"You showed up!" Larry exclaimed with a smile when I walked up to the jobsite the next morning. I looked around and noticed that the other guy who had worked with us the day before was absent. "Sometimes in life, all you have to do is show up," he said to me as we walked, shovel in hand, to continue digging a foundation. Again I tore into the ground, this time with a certain vengeance. The work was like the manifestation of the scream I wanted the universe to hear.

"I love working with people that know how to work," Larry said to me when we were done.

"I only know how to do things one way, and that's all-out," I answered.

Listen, Will, I'm not sure why you wanted to work in construction because I'm sure there are so many other things you can do. However, if you want to get serious in the construction business, how about you go full time with me and help me grow this business?"

I wanted to tell him that I had a looming court date ahead, but since I knew I was innocent and truly believed I would beat the case, I decided against it. The next thing I knew, Larry was teaching me AutoCAD and even got me a book to help me pick up the basics of computer-assisted designing. Our friendship quickly grew, as did our business. Flying planes had always been my dream, but I began to wonder if, once I got exonerated from the bogus rape charge, I would stay in construction.

The days dragged on as the date of my first hearing approached. I felt as if I was carrying a ton of bricks on my shoulders. I was in and out of court, in and out of George's office, in and out of this, and in and out of that. It was awful! My emotions would quench my appetite and I would break out in cold sweats. I was literally walking around like a zombie.

Preparing for my first hearing was surreal. I don't know how to express the feelings you go through when you wake up to go to court to face your accuser for the first time. I wondered if she would have the guts to look at me. I imagined her silently mouthing the words "I'm sorry" to me. A flicker of hope ignited inside me that she would recant her whole testimony once she saw me. I had taken her in when she didn't have a place to live. Sure, we had our arguments, but I hoped that she would remember me for who I really was and end this charade.

However, Jill didn't do that. She didn't say "I'm sorry" and she didn't say I did it. She didn't say anything because she never showed up. The emotional rollercoaster I was on was in high gear. I had so many questions for my lawyer. "What does that mean? Will the case be dismissed? They must know she's lying now, right?"

Unfortunately, my questions were answered when the judge postponed the trial.

The second time we were supposed to appear in court, Jill was a no-show as well. Again, the case was continued because again the prosecution wasn't ready. The only relief to my frustration was that Jill, true to her erratic and inconsistent behavior, had not shown up for either court hearing.

When Jill didn't show up at the third hearing, the judge opted not to place her under arrest for contempt. Instead, the trial was dismissed for lack of evidence. I was ecstatic! I hugged everyone within arm's reach. Karma had prevailed, and although I had not been found "not guilty," the possibility of me going to jail on that trumped-up charge was over. It took six long months of my life from the time George had called me to the time it was dismissed.

I was happy to be free. Of course, I hadn't gone to jail but I'm referring to being free to enjoy my life again without debilitating thoughts ruining my happiness. I was more than content with letting the whole thing fade away as if it were a very bad dream - a forgettable, bitter, and disappointing chapter in my life. I was living in Florida at the time. Life was great! Everything was coming together again.

Although I liked working with Larry and we were growing his construction company, my heart was in aviation. I knew that with my case being public record, I would have to admit to the charge pressed on me. In order to get my job back I had to re-interview again. As fate would have it, everyone that I had to speak with was a female, including the head of operations and the human resources director. I had to shamefully tell them why I had requested the leave of absence and the result of the case. The fact that the case was dismissed because of lack of evidence, rather than my being acquitted, didn't sit well with the women who had the authority to re-hire me.

"What guarantee do I have that you are not going to rape one of my flight attendants or female pilots, Mr. Smith?" the assistant chief asked during my interview with her. Apparently the disgrace of being charged for rape would follow me like a dark shadow.

"I know this stigma will stay with me as long as I live," I said holding back the tears in my eyes. "I have gone through hell trying to clear my name but, believe me, I am innocent. I am incapable of such an abusive and despicable act. Rest assured that every female that I will ever encounter would not have a reason to fear me. I guarantee you." I don't know how to fully explain the feeling of having to apologize for something heinous you have never done but it's a mixture of sorrow, anger, and shame.

She glared at me with the piercing look of a woman committed to safeguarding the wellbeing of her female employees. After a long moment considering what I had said, she rose and walked to the window in her office overlooking the tarmac.

"Very well, Mr. Smith, you are re-hired," she said turning around. "But at the slightest indication of improper conduct on your part, sexual or otherwise from anyone in my team, you'll go from flying airplanes to driving taxi cabs; or worse."

When they hired me back, they based me out of Beckley Bluefield, West Virginia. My life slowly crept back to the normalcy it once had, except for the fact that I was much more appreciative of it. Life was great. Until one day, as I was leaning against one of the cars of a luggage train at the tarmac of Boston's Logan Airport, George Hughes called.

"Will, are you sitting down?" he asked in a somber tone. "I received a formal communication from court this morning notifying me that you have been re-indicted."

"Damn it, George, are you fucking serious!"

"I'm sorry, Will, but I am."

Again! Not again, please! I wanted to run away from everything. Escape. Cross the border. Go to Brazil, or Venezuela, or anywhere to hide and get asylum to avoid the impending feeling of doom and gloom that rushed through my head. I had just gotten my job and life back after a lot of humiliation and an enormous effort on my part. I felt drained and angry. I was desperately seeking a way out of all this chaotic mess. This was crazy.

"Will, unfortunately, I have some more bad news."

I stayed quiet.

"The private investigator that you hired, the one that interviewed all of your witness, including Jill, has killed himself," George said.

I looked up to the sky, hoping a plane would come down on me and end it all in one swift instant. "What are you saying George?"

"His wife had a brain tumor and her doctor had given her six months to live. Apparently her pain and agony was more than he could handle so, with his regulation pistol, he shot and killed her. Then he killed himself."

I didn't have the time or inclination to mourn for the only person who had the testimonies that could help me. "So, what does that mean for my case?"

"It means that, most likely, none of those testimonies will be allowed should this case go to trial," he answered.

"And what are the odds that the case goes to trial? I mean, it got dismissed not too long ago."

"The state is not going to re-indict you if they aren't positive that it will go to trial this time. I'm sorry, Will, but I need to know when you will be able to turn yourself in again."

So there I was, back to square one all over again. This time it was worse. Jill had finally showed up to testify against me.

Chapter 7

We Go to Trial

Jury selection is a part of the trial process that doesn't make a lot of headlines, nor does it take up much airtime in a television court drama or a movie. However, in my case, the jury selection process was incredibly important. Unfortunately for me, it foretold how my case was going to be handled.

In "normal" cases, one panel of perspective jurors to choose from is more than enough. However, we went through three entire panels of prospective jurors, and the proceedings got a bit loud and confrontational. The prosecuting attorney looks to select jurors who would be more empathetic to the plaintiff, while the defense looks for someone who they hope would be more inclined to give the benefit of the doubt to the defendant. In a rape case, such as mine, naturally the prosecution wanted women or fathers with daughters. We were looking for men who might have known what it was like to have a good time and brush shoulders with girls who like to party.

The first time my lawyer, George Hill, motioned to strike a potential juror, was also the first time I took real notice of Judge Evelyn Hill. The juror in question was a mother of three daughters and by her attire, we considered her to be a conservative. Judge Hill dismissed my attorney's request and we later found out that she had selected that woman to be part of the jury.

"This is a bit uncharacteristic as to how these proceeding typically go," George said to me. "But then again, Judge Hill has a reputation of doing what she wants."

Judge Hill continued to exert her authority and summarily dismiss most of what my lawyer said. Had it not been to my potential detriment, it would have been fascinating to me to see how she was able to subject everyone to her own brand of justice. After five women had been selected and zero men, George and I really started to worry. One particular woman was greeted warmly by Judge Hill. George stood up and moved to strike her from the jury, which raised Judge Hill's ire.

"I want to make something clear before we proceed with this potential juror. She and I attend the same church." I groaned. "We also sing in the same choir together. Now Matilda, would your relationship with me make you prejudiced to Mr. Smith in any way, shape, or form?"

"No, your honor," Matilda answered with a straight face. "God forbid, you know I would never show prejudice against anyone."

Judge Hill smiled at her and then her smile dissipated as she turned to look at us. "The court sees no reason why we should remove this potential juror from the pool."

The bias was so blatant that it got to the point that the prosecutor, whose job it was to find me guilty, backed off and even started to talk to the judge on our behalf. The prosecutor said that allowing some of the people we wanted on the jury was all right with the state. However, the judge had her own jury in mind and was adamant about it.

At one point, I went to say something, only to be reprimanded harshly by Judge Hill. "Mr. Smith, this is my courtroom," she said. "I will decide who is fit to be a juror in this case, is that clear?"

We were dumbstruck. Could this even happen? I continuously looked around for help from a bailiff, my lawyer, and even the prosecutor, but no one would dare stand up against Judge Hill in her courtroom. My high-priced attorney had no answers for me. He didn't know what else to do. He fought tooth and nail to balance the jury but the judge had the final say.

It took a day and a half to select the twelve people who would decide my fate. The jury was comprised of nine women and three men. Three men with daughters. However, unbeknownst to me at the time, there would be a 13th juror who had already made up her mind about my guilt. She wore a black robe and held a gavel.

Chapter 8

The Deck is Stacked

I was grateful for the many gestures of love and affection that were expressed to me in the days leading up to the trial. Even some people that I had not seen in a long time showed their support for me one way or another. True friends, people you have real relationships with, rise to the occasion as the word spreads that you are in trouble. That's when you realize what kind of seed you have been sowing. True friendship cannot be faked for too long or bought; it's as genuine as the intentions of the heart.

"Hey man, I'm on my way up."

"I appreciate it bro, I really do, but no sense in coming all the way up here..."

Rob Howard, who I had been talking to on the phone, cut me off. "Are you serious? I don't care what you say, Will, I'm going there to support you 100 percent of the way."

I had known Rob since high school. We became friends as soon as we met and stayed close after we graduated. We even started a couple of businesses together. I couldn't tell Rob how much it meant to me that he would travel up from Florida to sit in a courtroom just to let me know that he was there for me. Although I was blessed to have a strong support group of friends and family, I also had many so-called friends, who just disappeared during that time. I didn't get any phone calls, emails, texts, or anything from a lot of people.

"Just keep your head up, Will, you're going to beat this charge and I want to be there when you do. I'll see you soon."

My sister Nancy also stood steadfast at my side. "I'm with you, Will, no matter what."

"It's going to be all right, bro," Andrew said to me. "Good things happen to good people and you're a good person. "Most days anyway." He always knew how to make someone smile even when they didn't feel like it.

The memories of my loved ones showing up in court would be etched in my soul to give me the strength to endure whatever lay ahead. People who never forget you are those who really matter in life. They are the ones who carry you across the seemingly endless walk through the desert. So it was, with a trembling heart, but a feeling of support, that I went to court for the first day of my trial.

With the courtroom full, waiting for the judge, I glanced again and nodded appreciatively the contingency of people that came to support me. I noticed that Jill's father was not present; only her mother. Her side was much smaller and less vocally supportive than mine. I then looked at Jill for the first time since the incident happened. She was looking straight ahead, as if not daring to make eye contact with me. I wanted her to look at me. I swear if I could just talk to her for five minutes I could convince her to end this farce.

"All rise." A bailiff's baritone voice filled the courtroom. "Judge Evelyn Hill is presiding." The rustle of clothes, shuffling of feet, and creaking of benches and chairs was heard as Hill took her seat with a sympathetic look at Jill. When we all sat down George put his hand on my shoulder, as if to say that everything was going to be all right.

Then my trial began. I can't fully recall what the district attorney said, but hearing me being called a rapist in court was enough to get my ire burning. As instructed by my attorney, I looked at the jury with as passive of a look that I could give, to remind them that I was a real person and not the monster being portrayed. My eyes locked with several jurors but only momentarily, as they quickly averted their eyes from mine.

When it was finally his turn, George got up from his seat, buttoned up one of the buttons of his dark gray suit, and walked to the center of the courtroom. His voice was confident and his remarks were measured. He explained to the jury that we were going to present facts that an adult woman voluntarily went over to my house, that she had gotten into bed with me, that consensual sex was had, that it wasn't the first time she had had consensual sex in my home, that she wasn't a powerless, innocent victim, that I was a pilot in good standing, that I had never been in trouble with the law, and that I did not commit a crime that night.

When he sat next to me I was proud to have him representing me. I looked again at the jury, to try to read their faces, but had no idea as to which lawyer convinced them more. The prosecution called its first witness and we were off. He began to ask questions to well-coached witnesses. Then it started to get really weird. As one of his witnesses was on the stand, Judge Hill asked a question that should have come from the prosecuting attorney.

"I object your honor," George said as he stood up.

"Overruled," she answered. "You may answer my question," she said to the witness. George sat down and made a note on his yellow legal sized notepad. Judge Hill, apparently not getting the answer she wanted, asked another question.

"Your honor, I object," George said again as he stood, "You're leading the witness." He said with a hint of exasperation in his voice.

"I want to make sure that the truth gets out," she answered, looking at the jury. "Overruled." My lawyer put his hands up over his head and looked around as if gesturing to everyone to see what was going on. A judge, sworn to be impartial and uphold the law, was actually doing the job of the prosecuting attorney. "Mr. Hughes, I will not suffer these antics in my courtroom. Is that understood?"

"Understood, judge" George said solemnly and sat back down.

"What the fuck is going on?" I whispered to him.

When he looked at me, his look of defeat, this early into my trial, froze my limbs. "I don't think she is going to let me defend you properly, Will."

During the lunch break, as I sat with my mother and other supporters, we were all speaking as if we were sedated. The wind had been taken out of our sails.

"She is evil," my mother said. "I can see why the North Carolina judicial standards committee has reprimanded her for unfairness and impropriety."

That got the conversation going about how the trial was turning out in a way none of us had expected. "In complaints to the Judicial Standards Commission," my mother said, "lawyers have claimed that she berated, belittled, and mocked them. They say she's even made racially insensitive remarks from the bench."

My mother was right, but then again, moms usually are. Judge Hill had earned a reputation for being unprofessional, racist, unfair, and one sided. These are the types of remarks she has said; these remarks are in court transcripts and documents in the state of North Carolina:

2000

- "What you need to leave is your penis," to a domestic assault defendant regarding bail at his bond hearing.
- "When you talk to the jury, start off the morning in your big boy voice," to defense attorney Andrew McCoppin in court.
- "I know he's just the 'token' sitting at the table with you," to attorney George Hunt in the courtroom about his partner Octavious White, a black defense attorney.

2001

- "You are disrespectful and contemptuous," to Durham defense attorney Keith Bishop during a trial.
- "You are kind of incompetent. Don't you think a good lawyer would know about that?" to Kerry Larsen, a Washington, D.C. defense attorney during a trial.
- "I haven't heard anything you've said so far to suggest you even have a heart," to Kerry Larsen in court.
- "You'll probably see 13 collective people throwing up at your comments," to defense attorney Mark Simeon, referring to herself and the trial jury.

2002

- "Get the hell out of my way. It's been a long time since I've shoved a man's balls," to deputy Brian

Bowers while leaving the courtroom after a trial.
- "Apparently the Asian community doesn't have the equivalent of a Rev. Al Sharpton to represent them," to a robbery defendant during his trial.
- "If you truly want to make amends, you don't walk into this courtroom wearing a gold bracelet, a gold ring, and a nice suit," to a defendant who was a stockbroker accused of embezzlement.

2003
- "You could shovel horse manure or mop up blood and guts at the ER," to a defendant in a worthless check trial about repaying his debt.
- "Suggest to the jury to consider a different kind of stud – Mel Gibson," during a crucial testimony about construction studs.

2004
- "You have no black pride. I have more black pride than you do," to a black defendant in court.
- "Do you know what they called my daughter in high school? She was called a nigger lover. You have no respect for your race, that's the truth," to three black defendants at trial.

It was also said that she called people racial slurs, beat up on defense attorneys, dismissed witnesses, and showed bias.

"Yep, that's her all right," said Andrew, who besides having had sexual encounters with Jill, was listed as one of my witnesses. He knew my family and me since childhood and was eager to testify on my behalf as to the integrity of my character and his relationship with Jill.

"George, we can't have that judge," mom insisted. "Isn't there any way we can get another judge assigned to Will's case?"

"That's almost like pushing water uphill, Mrs. Smith," George explained politely. "However, I am documenting everything that transpires in that court and, trust me, I will use it against that judge in the blink of an eye if I get a chance."

* * * *

When the trial continued, Judge Hill got worse. The DA just had to summon a witness to the stand and ask a question or two before she took over his line of questioning. This was the judge, who is supposed to ensure that I got a fair trial, the whole innocent until proven guilty system of justice that everyone is entitled to, asking questions of the witnesses to ensure that I got convicted. I would look over at the jury to see if they were swallowing this load of crap. Unfortunately, they appeared to shake their heads in agreement with every question the judge asked. Then I remembered *dear sister Matilda*, one of the judge's friends, had access to the other jurors. When someone in a position of authority crosses the limits of his or her office and blatantly disregards the consequences of his actions, that person is assuming the place that only belongs to a deity.

When it was George's turn to cross examine the defenses witnesses, the judge would strike certain questions from needing to be answered. The instances of misuse of her position of power were so many and so obvious to all those present in the courtroom that every one of us commented about them during breaks and every time we had a chance.

I later found out that my mother got so nervous about the whole thing that she got up and went to the bathroom to throw up. This was taking a toll on all of us. We were uneasy, on edge, and not confident about the final outcome of this whole mess.

The next day, the court episode was marred by continued interruptions by a moody, authoritative and disrespectful judge who discouraged the voicing of any opinions other than her own. It was our turn to provide my defense and George had put Andrew on the stand. He had just testified that he had had sexual relations with Jill when Judge Hill interrupted George's line of questioning.

"This is my case, and I will not allow you to fool my jury," she said. "You guys fly together, so you are obviously biased toward Mr. Smith." Then she looked at the jury. "You are to strike each and every one of this witness' remarks. He is obviously biased toward the defendant and I will not allow this charade to influence your decision."

"Can you do that?" I said, totally out of turn and process. I had been holding so much in that it escaped my lips before I realized.

Judge Hill looked at me with venom, as if she had baited a rat with cheese and had finally caught him in her trap. "You will not disrespect this courtroom, sir. This is not your party house where you can carry on with whatever shenanigans you want, Mr. Smith." George gave me a look as if to tell me to just keep my mouth shut. "To answer your question, though, yes I can do that. I can also hold you in contempt and send you to jail for the night if you make any rude outburst."

I was pissed. Just as George predicted, we weren't able to use any of the information gathered by the private investigator I had to hire because the detective wouldn't interview anyone on my behalf. All of the ammunition I thought I had to clear my name was either not allowed to be presented or curtailed by the intimidating, power hungry monster sitting on the bench.

Later on, when George was trying to get the testimony from Carlton, who worked with me at the same airline, George had had about enough. "Your honor, I want to make it noted on record that I object to you disallowing my questions to be answered."

"If you keep objecting and questioning my decisions, Mr. Hughes, I will find you in contempt of court and you'll spend the night in jail," she yelled. "For the last time, this is my court and my trial. Is that understood?"

I swear, she loved telling us that it was her court. She must have said it twenty times during my trial. She was so imposing that she even disallowed any of my female witnesses to take the stand. My freedom was at stake and my lawyer could not properly defend me. It was ludicrous.

Even the prosecutor noticed I wasn't getting a fair trial. He started to back off from questioning in response to the abusive behavior displayed by the judge. She then started cross examining me from the bench, asking me direct questions in violation of established court procedure!

"I'm fed up with this, Will," George whispered to me.

Drawing on his experience and legal instincts from years of litigation, George realized that we were in a sinking ship and there was little hope of winning this with Judge Hill presiding.

The next morning, he brought friends of his into the courtroom that included other lawyers who he worked with, as well as a police captain, as witnesses to the injustice that was being committed.

"I'm doing this, Will, because this judge is out of control," George told me. "If I continue objecting and raising any more questions, she's going to place me in contempt and that will only make matters worse."

That morning Judge Hill decided to show up late, arriving at the bench past 10:30 a.m., although we had been summoned to be there at 8:30 a.m. Then she ordered lunch recess at 11:30 a.m., wasting not only our entire morning but also the taxpayers' money since nothing was accomplished until late in the afternoon.

When it was Jill's turn to get up on the stand, I looked at her intently as if to tell her, "What the hell are you doing up there? What are you up to? What's the purpose of all this?" She immediately started crying and visibly trying to make the jury feel sorry for her. She admitted to being drunk as part of her defense strategy to blame me for taking advantage of an intoxicated woman to satisfy my sexual desires.

"My family doesn't want to talk to me. They are ashamed of me. I feel dirty and rejected," she sobbed.

All the time I was thinking *How the fuck can you do this when you know perfectly well that you drove yourself to my house that night, got in my bed, stripped naked, went down on me, and practically coerced me to fuck you, you bitch!*

It was during that time that I discovered that Judge Hill denied us the right to present the rape kit that came up with negative results as evidence. She even refused to allow the fact that John was in the room with Jill after I returned from the kitchen that night as evidence because he wasn't in the courtroom himself to testify.

We were running out of time and out of options so, in a last-ditch effort to save the day, George asked me if I was willing to take the stand.

"I know you have a short fuse when other people try to put words in your mouth, Will," he said. "But due to the circumstances, and in the interest of providing the best possible outcome in your defense, I strongly recommend that you testify on your behalf."

So it was, with immense trepidation that I prepared to take the stand.

Chapter 9

The Verdict

"My son is just about ready to lose the rest of his life here," my mother told George, as if scolding him while we sat in a meeting room with other supporters. "You have to help him get out of this mess."

"Trust me, Mrs. Smith, I am doing everything in my power to get clear him of this charge," George explained to my mother respectfully. "It's just that this judge is blatantly disregarding all the canons of judicial procedures. In all my years of practicing law, I never experienced something like this."

I looked at them both, hoping for a look or a nod of reassurance. However, not only they, but everyone in the room seemed to not want to look anyone in the eye. It reminded me of being part of a team at halftime that was losing 50-0. What can the coach possibly say?"

Someone knocked twice but I didn't look up. My head was in my hands as I heard a female saying, "We are ready to continue; the judge is here." As everyone filed out of the room, some of them looked at me with a half-smile. I nodded to show them that I appreciated their effort, even though we all began to realize what the only outcome could be. Judge Hill had not allowed some of my witnesses to testify on my behalf during the proceedings. The ones that she allowed, she told the jurors to disregard their testimonies because we were friends. Of course I would bring friends up to the stand; who the hell else would I bring!

When it was my turn to take the stand I had so many emotions going through me. I wanted to just scream at the judge to stop interfering and just preside over the trial fairly and I wanted to scream at Jill for making me go through this.

"William, remember," George said to me as we sat at the defendant's table. "Don't show any anger. We don't want the jury to think that you fly off the handle."

"But this judge . . . "

George held his hand up and interrupted me. "I know. Trust me, a lot of people know. But this is not the time for you to worry about the judge. The jury needs to be your only focus right now. I've been around you for a while now and you can make anyone like you. That's the William I need on the stand. Got it?"

I breathed deeply, knowing that I might have to hold my tongue even more. I hoped that I could.

After some trivial conversation, George, who was already standing, said aloud, "I will now call William Smith to the stand." He looked at me and gave me a reassuring nod, visible enough for everyone to see. As if to say, "now we'll sort this thing out." I thought I would be scared, but I approached the witness stand confident because all I had to do was tell the truth.

I don't recall all that was said, but the entire transcript is here if anyone would like to read it.

What I do remember is, that as I was answering a question, Judge Hill interrupted me. "Would you do me a big favor and stop wiggling," she said.

Another time, again, as I was answering a question, she interrupted me. "Would you please speak clearer? With all the wiggling and mumbling it's hard to understand what you are saying."

She had never addressed anyone in that manner during the trial. She was obviously trying to break whatever connection she thought I was building with the jury. I looked right at her, "Yes, ma'am."

Another time, as I was answering an open-ended question about the fact that she could have slept in another room, she interrupted. "Sir, I remind you that you have a simple job. Just answer the questions that are asked. Can you do that?" she said as if talking to a child.

"Mr. Hughes," she said at one point, interrupting my lawyer when he was phrasing a question to me, "If you'd kindly refrain from asking leading questions, the court would appreciate it."

As I turned to address my attorney, she took in a loud breath. "Thank you," she said condescendingly, as if I had been rude or something.

I was able to tell my story, although in bits and pieces due to the interruptions from the judge who acted more like the prosecuting attorney. I shared with the jury that Jill did in fact drive to my house at 4 a.m. and that she was drunk. I also told them that Jill went up to my room on her own volition. I was able to say what I knew to be true and hoped that it would be enough.

"Your honor," George had said after my interview on the stand, "I would like to redirect to Mr. Carlton."

"You had your chance with Mr. Carlton, Mr. Hughes." she said.

"Yes, your honor, but I believe I have a legal right to redirect. Mr. Carlton spoke to Jill the next day and had never mentioned rape to him and I think it is an important..."

"The jury will disregard the comments of Mr. Hughes as it is hearsay. The court feels that you had your opportunity to ask all of your questions. Request denied." Then she said some other stuff that I didn't pay attention to because of my outrage.

During the closing arguments, Judge Hill interrupted my attorney repeatedly. At one point she said, "Stick with the facts, sir. That is your opinion. The justice system does not make decisions based on personal opinions."

Although my attorney did all he could, without the testimonies of several key character references and the statements obtained by the private investigator who I had hired, who later killed himself, I felt as if I held up a pocketknife at a gunfight. When the DA gave his closing arguments, instead of interrupting him, she actually elaborated for him, as if making sure that the jury understood what he said!

When both cases had been presented, she turned to the jury, "I must instruct you about an important facet of the law. It is implied in law that if someone has been drinking alcohol, anyone that has sex with that person needs to be found guilty because they cannot intelligently consent."

I leaned to George's ear and whispered, "What the fuck is that? Does that mean that if two people have some drinks and they have sex, the man is suddenly a rapist?" He just nodded his agreement but didn't look at me. I didn't blame him. What could he say to me? The score was now 100 to zero.

"All rise," a bailiff bellowed as Judge Hill rose. She walked away and when the door shut behind her, I felt as if my freedom had been slammed.

* * * *

I don't recall much after that. It was as if I was experiencing an out of body experience. I had been a pilot living the kind of life that many men would kill for. But at that moment, I don't think anyone on earth would have traded places with me. I went to the bathroom and threw up and then paced non-stop as I smoked one cigarette after another. Before I knew it, more than three hours had passed and we were summoned back to the courtroom.

The jury had reached a verdict.

It is ironic all the things you take for granted right when you know you are about to lose them. I wonder if those who had walked to their deaths by hanging or by an injection of needles felt the same way I did. For the first time ever I focused on the curve of the courtroom benches and found them to be quite elegant. I also noticed the intricate detail that the carpenter who designed the first bench of its kind had created. The first bench must have been quite impressive for so many others of its kind to be manufactured.

I felt as if I heard someone in another parallel existence shout, "dead man walking" as I took my time making my way to my seat. The bailiffs looked at me with pity as if letting me know that I got screwed. The courtroom was not nearly as talkative as in prior times. My supporters had grown in numbers, but fearing the worst, they were quiet. Jill's supporters, who were very few to start, were only her mother and another lady. Judge Hill walked into the quiet courtroom with her now customary pompous manner and the bailiff's voice seemed far away as he ordered everyone to rise.

"Has the jury reached a verdict?" she asked, confident in the result she was expecting. Judge Evelyn Hill had become my nemesis, my executioner, the personification of a blind justice system gone bad and capable of inflicting as much harm behind a supposedly honorable cloak as the lowest hit man from a neighborhood street gang. She had systematically and viciously destroyed all my defense arguments while exalting and highlighting anything she could to reinforce the prosecution's standing. I was angry, anxious, and afraid.

"We have, your honor," answered the female lead juror, handing the verdict over to the judge. I wasn't sure if I imagined it but I thought I saw Judge Hill smirk slightly when she read the verdict silently to herself before handing the paper back to the juror.

"Very well, how do you find the accused?" she asked in a light, almost melodic tone.

This was it, the moment of truth. I couldn't close my eyes but I couldn't see anything either.

"We the jury find the defendant, William Beach Smith, guilty of 2nd degree rape."

I heard my niece Katie gasp loudly followed by cries of "No!" Others began to shout as I closed my eyes in sorrow and disbelief at what my life had just turned to. My niece started to cry loudly and I turned and looked back at my supporters with a thought of telling them not to cry, but all they saw was a stunned look on my face. Erick and Carlton got up and stomped out of the courtroom. I figured they didn't want anyone to see them show emotion. I made eye contact with Andrew and his face was expressionless; he had that deer-in-the-headlights glaze. Then I saw my mother crying, and her shoulders were moving up and down as if the sobs were racking her entire body.

"Bailiffs, please escort that young lady out of my courtroom" Judge Hill said, referring to my niece.

I turned away from my supporters, sorry for myself and sorry that I was putting them through this grief. I grabbed George's wrist, "I can't go to jail."

"I'm so sorry, Will," he said. "I don't know what else I could have done. I will do everything I can to fix this." He took a moment to gather himself and directed his attention to Judge Hill.

"Your honor, I request a recess and for sentencing in the morning so that my client can have the adequate time to put his affairs in order." He said loudly.

Judge Hill could barely conceal her annoyance to his request. "Request denied, Mr. Hughes. The court has spent enough time on this trial as it is. I will deliver my sentence now."

In a way I was happy that she said that. I just wanted to start the process of serving my time and getting over with it. Being that I had never been in trouble with the law, the standard time was 20-36 months in jail. I just wanted to get it over with.

Judge Hill directed her attention fully onto me. "Mr. Smith, I hereby sentence you to no less than 72 months and no more than 96 months at a state penitentiary." Again my supporters reacted emotionally at the imposed sentence. I wanted to ask George if she could do that but the question had been answered.

"Bailiff take Mr. Smith into custody immediately," She ordered.

"Your honor," George said, trying to get her attention as she stood up from the bench. "I request a moment for

Mr. Smith to say his farewells to his mother and family and hand them his valuables."

Judge Hill, standing now, stooped over to get close to the microphone. "Request denied. Bailiff!" With that she turned and left. It was the last time I would ever see her in person.

As the bailiff came to get me, George started to say something to him but the bailiff interrupted him. "Don't worry. I don't care what she said." He looked at me. "Go hug your loved ones, Mr. Smith. We'll wait for you."

I thanked him and went to my group who supported me throughout the trial. My mother ran up to me and told me all the reassuring words she could. I didn't have the words or the conviction in my voice to tell her that I would be okay so I just held on to her for a while. Then I tried to hug all of the people that had been there for me. The love they had for me was palpable; I even got patted on the back by other officers of the court who had realized that my trial had been conducted unjustly. I appreciated that they did that but it did nothing to console me. My freedom was gone. I was going to jail.

Chapter 10

Hell Part One

"What's going to happen now?" I managed to ask one of the bailiffs who had witnessed the proceedings and had always demonstrated empathy toward me.

"We'll take you downstairs to the jail and you will have to sit there and wait until the state has room and is ready to process you," he said in an even tone.

I was placed in a 6' x 6' cell with three other guys. I was so drained from the ordeal that all I wanted to do was to lay down somewhere and sleep. One of the guys said something to me and I told him that I wasn't in the mood to talk. I went to the latrine, took a roll of toilet paper and, still dressed in my double-breasted suit, used the toilet paper as a pillow. I lay down with my head under a bench. I closed my eyes and fell into a deep sleep.

"Wake up, Smith," a voice I had never heard before brought me back to my nightmare. "Hurry up. You are going to a holding cell before processing."

The holding cell was full of goons and rejects from society. When I was escorted in, one guy was throwing up in the toilet. Perhaps it was from the food he had been given or maybe he had been there so long that he was having withdrawals from his drug of choice. I didn't know and I didn't care. All I wanted to do was to lay down on the floor with a toilet paper pillow and forget this was even happening to me.

A couple of guys tried to be nice, but I wasn't in the mood to talk to anyone. I was grateful that there was a full roll of toilet paper in that overcrowded cell, though. I lay down and, I don't know if some of the guys did this on purpose or because the cell was so full but, people kicked me and stomped over me as they moved about. I had no fight in me though; all I wanted to do was crawl under a bench and sleep.

A commotion in the cell woke me up and I noticed a corrections officer handing out bags of food. He threw one at me. I grabbed it and turned away from him and the suddenly-too-loud people in the cell with me. I tried to get some sleep and just as I was about to drift off, two of the guys started to fight in the cell. When the corrections officer came to see why they were quarreling, one of the guys said that he didn't have enough to eat. I guess he wanted to take the other guy's food.

"Take my food and shut the fuck up," I said as I threw my untouched brown paper bag at him.

About 18 hours had gone by since the food incident and I began to realize that time was an expendable commodity in jail. I had not eaten in what seemed like two days, but I still wasn't hungry. There was no way I could eat in that nasty environment with that smelled of shit, piss, sweat, armpit, and vomit. I was in a state of full mental shut down.

"Smith, you're up for processing, get up," again, a voice I had never heard before woke me up. However, I was given a bit of good news. There was a room available where I could rest without anyone kicking me. Before getting transported to processing, I was reminded of my right to make one phone call. Surprisingly, the only number I could remember in my depleted memory bank was my ex-wife's, Shannon, the mother of my two sons.

"Will, where are you? The kids have been asking. Are you all right?" asked the sweetest voice I had heard in a long, long time. I knew I would not have been where I was if we had never divorced. I had never told her what I was going through because I was certain that I was going to beat the case and I didn't want to hear any unwarranted lectures. My heart broke for her and the kids.

"Shannon, you're not going to believe this, but I'm in jail."

"I'm a bit too far to bail you out. Do you want me to call someone . . ."

"I don't have a lot of time," I interrupted. It was clear to me that Shannon thought I was in jail for something simple. "I've been convicted of rape," I said.

"Wha. . . . Don't piss me off, Will. That's not funny," she answered. "What's going on?"

I tried to explain the situation but she kept asking questions and my time on the phone was running out so I asked her to call my mother for the full story. We ended the conversation with a rushed good-bye, not realizing it would be a while before we would speak to each other again. I knew that she would call my mom and get all the information and oddly enough, that gave me a small sense of comfort.

I didn't stay in that quiet cell for too long, though. After I got processed, which among other things means I was given prison clothes and they took all that I owned, I was going to be transferred to a maximum-security prison where I would be deprived of basic amenities and some of the blessings of life I had always taken for granted. They call the jail where I was processed, "The Wall." I would spend 28 days there before being moved.

I was put in a new pod while I waited, joining the general population. In this new pod the cells were full of wannabe gangsters and failed rappers. I'd always thought of them as jokes but I was in their world now and had to take them seriously. I realized that the level of criminals I was with had gotten dramatically more sinister from the ones that had stepped on me in the holding cell in the courthouse. I wondered how I would survive in this environment once they knew what I was in for, and that was everyone's way of starting a conversation, "What are you in for?" Actually, it sounded more like, "Watchoo in fo?"

I don't know if they took my silence as a guy that didn't give a shit or a guy that was scared shitless. I knew that I had to start interacting with some of them, though, if I was going to survive. We were given $40 a week to spend on things we needed but the other prisoners stole that from me regularly. I was constantly being harassed and had no interest in getting to know anyone or even speaking to any of the other prisoners.

"We all fam here," one of the black guys said to me, trying to get me to talk.

What the hell did I care about the so-called *fam*, which I later found out meant "family." I wasn't remotely related to any one of these shitheads incarcerated with me. They could all go fuck their "fams" for all I cared. All I wanted was to be left alone. *Alone*! Minutes slowly turned into hours and the hours slowly turned into days.

* * * *

"Hey, you!" a corrections officer said to me. "You're getting moved."

I couldn't get out of that cell fast enough. "Can I ask why I'm being moved?"

"Apparently your sister thinks you're going to kill yourself."

"What? Wha . . ."

"That sister of yours has called the sheriff's office over and over and over again. She told them that she feared for your life and that we needed to do something to protect you. So, you're going to solitary confinement."

Of course, what my sister had meant was that she was afraid for my safety, believing that with my charge, I would be in physical or maybe even mortal danger. She told them that she feared for my life, which translated by the narrow mindset of the prison system, meant I was suicidal. She meant the best for me but didn't realize that she had just done me a big disservice.

The first thing they did was strip me of my prison clothes and put me in covering made of paper, It was like wearing a paper bag and it stripped me of more than clothing, it stripped what little dignity I had been trying to hold on to. Next, I was thrown in a cell in the basement of the jail with nothing to read, no windows, strong lights that stayed on 24/7 and surveillance cameras to watch my every move as I was on suicide watch. If I had wanted to kill myself, there wasn't a damn thing in the room to do it with. I have never felt that alone in my life. There was nothing to connect me to anything or anyone. All I wanted to do was sleep. I had nothing to read, no distractions from my own mind so I tried to put myself in a kind of a sleep coma in order to make it through the agonizing minutes and hours. I was there for two extremely long days with just my thoughts, a metal bed, and the occasional drop-off of disgusting food. I curled up in a ball on the floor most of the time as it was more comfortable than the cold metal cot. I didn't have a view of the outside world and lost track of day or night. If I stayed there much longer, I really would have considered killing myself!

They moved me again but at least this time I got a thin mattress to sleep on and a blanket. I felt like I won the lottery! I still didn't want to eat, talk, or make any friends, though. The following day I was allowed access to a phone. I was finally able to talk to my kids. The sound of their voices was the prettiest thing I had ever heard. I also got to talk to my mom, who was staying at my house, and two of my buddies, Erik and Carlton, who happened to be there when I made the call.

"Carlton, this is hell, man. I will never get used to this shit," I confessed.

"Hang in there, Will. We are not going to stop until you're a free man again, brother," he said in an effort to give me strength and encouragement.

They had no idea what this was like. I was a guy used to flying though clouds and blue skies. Now I was allowed to go out into a narrow passage way between buildings where the sky was barely visible for a miserable hour two days a week. The rest of the time I was in my cell where all I could do was listen to the sounds of prison life. Three men were executed while I was in there and I could hear them each screaming and crying and begging for their lives as they were dragged down for their final minutes on earth; the sound of nightmares. I could hear men having sex with each other, brutal, animal cries of a different kind. The first chance I got to buy anything. I bought the earplugs they sell you in jails. Small relief from the noises of the night.

* * * *

"Smith, get up, you are being transferred," a faceless uniform said one particularly cold day. I followed him, expecting to go to another cell, thinking that maybe my sister was still giving the sheriff's office hell. However, I realized that we were heading out of the jail. Before reaching the exit, the corrections officer was approached by a captain who said something to him that I couldn't hear. The corrections officer looked back with pity and escorted me into the visiting room.

In this room, visitors could only talk to prisoners through a six-inch thick glass with a telephone. I smiled when I saw that my sister Nancy and my mother had come to visit me. They had visited before and each time tried to cheer me up, but this time they had a different look on their faces, one of sorrow.

"Will, your dad died." My mother said and began to sob quietly along with Nancy, who was trying to be strong.

My dad had been battling cancer and now he was gone. I would not have a chance to say goodbye, hold his hand or see his face ever again. It was impossible to process.

I wanted to hug them and cry with them, but the only thing my hands could touch was a plastic phone and cold, thick glass. It was one of the most helpless feelings

I have ever experienced. I didn't know how to process what I was feeling. My emotions, which I had pushed down during my stay in jail, got the best of me. I loved my dad and recalled the great times we had together joking around and playing with train sets, but I think I cried more than anything because I couldn't be of support to my mother and sister. The loss of my father pierced the numbness that had cloaked me since my guilty verdict.

Immediately after that visit, the guards handcuffed me, shackled my feet, and put me in the back of a cop car and brought me to central prison.

During this 28-day processing, I had been transferred so many times I was beginning to feel like a piece of furniture that you don't know where to put, but are not ready to get rid of yet. My self-esteem had dropped down to zero, just like the cold February weather. Somehow the snow crept inside the cell and the cold just made matters worse. I was in a black hole of depression without room for emotion. Throughout my time there I was subjected to an endless array of tests, psychological evaluations, blood and urine testing, sex education, physical exams, you name it. I even took tests to help determine where they were going to send me. I was told they were going to send me to Nash County Prison because, based on my conviction, it would be better for me there.

Nash County was only a 45-minute drive from where we were. However, as with everything else in the prison system, the trip there took forever. We were dragged out at 6:20 am and tossed into the back of a school bus.

We made several stops at other institutions, each time dropping off or picking up other prisoners. We even made a few stops in the middle of nowhere for long periods of time for no apparent reason other than maybe milking the state for more money being that the guards, I assumed, were paid hourly. The drive-turned-epic-journey was incredibly frustrating as we were forced to remain sitting down, shackled for almost an entire day.

The driver took Highway 98 on the way to Nash County, and I was given a brown paper bag that concealed a peanut butter and jelly sandwich and a carton of orange juice. As I began eating my sandwich, I realized that I recognized the neighboring terrain. I knew exactly where we were and wondered to myself if I was going to see familiar sites as we passed. Sure enough, looming out of the dark, like a ghost from a distant past, I saw my house, the place where I used to live in, where my kids had lived. Once we passed by it I turned to see it fade from my sight. Yes, that was the place where it all started, where Jill had falsely accused me of raping her. I wondered when and if I would ever see it again.

Chapter 11

Nash Prison – Maximum Security

The sergeant that brought me to Nash pulled me aside and in a hushed tone said. "Listen man, you got railroaded. A lot of people know it. You don't belong in there so do yourself a favor. Protect yourself. Get a knife if you can."

Maximum security prison is no joke. Being in prison is just about the opposite of living. You merely exist as a faceless number stripped of all your dignity, identity, and self-worth. In prison, you must adapt in order to survive. The population of inmates was generally made up of black guys and white guys, with a small defiant Hispanic group thrown in the middle.

When I first was escorted into the pod I would be staying at, all of the inmates were in their cells. I was walking in with four other new prisoners and the tier went crazy. People started to spit at us, forcing us to walk in the center of the hallway. I saw some of the black guys, dicks in hand, masturbating and trying to hit us with their semen.

"Oh shit, I'm fucking that one right there!"

"Welcome to hell, white boy!"

"You gonna suck some dick tomorrow!"

"Fuck, more black meat!"

Everything that was said was meant to intimidate and test us. After taking a look at the jerk-off crew, I just kept looking straight ahead. I was scared shitless, but I tried to walk cool enough to not show it. I had to find a way to protect myself, to protect my ass, literally! I thought about sharks and how they have adapted over millions of years to still thrive.

The following morning, I opted not to go to breakfast because I knew the food would be terrible, but also because I didn't want to meet anyone. However, a few prisoners came to my cell to visit me. They tried to befriend me and told me that it would take about a week or two for my commissary to be set up and that, in the meantime, if I needed anything I could reach out to them and they would help me. I looked them in the eye and told them I appreciated it, but I knew their game. That's how they get you. They do you favors in the beginning but then you owe them and for those little favors in the beginning, you might owe them favors in return for years.

Going to jail for rape almost guarantees that your incarceration will be worse than most other inmates. The only people that are looked upon as being worse are child molesters. The racial divide in prison is real, especially in the south, where I was. As soon as I realized I had no control of how long I was going to be incarcerated, my survival instinct kicked into high gear and I began studying and analyzing those around me and evaluating how best to blend into my surroundings.

The first day I was able to buy from the commissary, I was sitting Indian-style outside of my cell with a bag of potato chips and other things I had bought to eat when a large bald white guy came up to me.

"Give me that," he said menacingly. He looked around, I assumed to check if any guards were in view. "Now." His muscles were easily defined even under all the tattoos he sported. I'm not a small guy, I stand at six feet and at that time I weighed in at a healthy and fit 210 lbs. I wasn't the biggest guy in there for sure, but I certainly wasn't the smallest. I didn't know what to do. It was all happening so fast. Do I make a stand there and fight him and let him know that I won't let him rob me? If I do, will I get in trouble for fighting and possibly extend my stay, even if I was defending myself?

He took the initiative and grabbed what I had from my hands with his left hand. With his right hand he punched me in my upper left torso, near my shoulder. It knocked me on my back, pain jolting throughout my upper body. "Welcome to prison, bitch!"

I stayed there on the floor, scared to see if anyone else had seen that exchange and if they had, would they try to do that to me next. I sat up to see that no one had witnessed it. However, I had the suspicion that this guy was going to be a real problem. I didn't want to join the gang of skinheads for protection, the black guys wouldn't take me in, and the Hispanics were too few in numbers to provide much help even if they wanted to. I was fucked unless I figured something out.

That night I realized that my best recourse was to find a way to be useful to every guy there, regardless of his ethnicity. As the days lurched on I witnessed more of the black jerk-off crew masturbating and throwing their loads all over the place. I also witnessed repeated beatings of inmates by the guards. The guards liked to tell you something once and if they had to tell you again, they would beat the crap out of you. Obedience was key. I saw the effects of inmates who had been beaten by other inmates more often than I saw the actual beat downs, but I did see plenty of beat downs. The worst thing you could do there was to be a snitch. It didn't matter what ethnicity you were, if you squealed to a corrections officer, even your own people would beat the hell out of you. I saw a supposed snitch get beaten and sliced to death with a modified chair leg that was converted into a makeshift sword. His blood stained the floor for weeks.

I was managing to do a decent job of flying below the radar and outside of the normal shit everyone got. I didn't get much more. I had begun opening up to people and realized that not all of the inmates were animals. I figured that most people wanted to just do their time and get back to their loved ones, however, the system brought out the worst in some and whether you liked it or not, sometimes you had to answer violence with violence.

I was trying to survive this hell without it changing who I was but the "system" began to take its toll on me. I fell into a deep depression and was starting to feel a righteous anger swell inside of me that would surely take me down the road of physical aggression. Realizing this would only make matters worse by extending my sentence and possibly even putting me on death row for killing an inmate, I decided to seek psychiatric counseling. He looked exactly how I thought he would. He was short, thin, and balding. He had a horrible hairstyle with about seven hairs that he combed over the top of his head. He wore iron-rimmed glasses and he had an uneven mustache. I soon got in an argument with him when he told me to attend a rape program.

"Why the hell would I?" I asked.

"Because, Mr. Smith, it will help you to deal with your issues and . . ."

I cut him off. "I didn't rape anybody! I am not going to concede to doing something I didn't do just because you think I did it!"

"Mr. Smith, I see that you are upset. Let me just say that this program has helped many inmates."

"Maybe it has, but I also hear that some of these idiots get so sexually aroused that they actually start jerking off right there!"

The psychiatrist picked up his glasses and looked through one of the lenses and started to wipe it with a cloth. "That does happen on occasion, but that's not the norm." He put his glasses back on while I relaxed my breathing.

"Tell me how you see the world right now, Mr. Smith," he asked, and then gave me a well-rehearsed smile.

"Life sucks for me right now doctor, but what pisses me the most is the fact that I don't belong here. I am not a criminal; I have always been a law-abiding citizen. I never had a record before this bullshit." As soon as I said that, I realized he must have heard those words a thousand times before.

Although I thought it was useless for me to talk to him, he told me that he would see if he could get me a job. That would keep me out of harm's way for parts of the day and keep my mind occupied. True to his word and due to my evaluation, I got a job at the print shop for government-funded activities in the state of North Carolina. My starting pay $05 cents an hour. There were raises for time on the job and some of the guys were making a whopping $028 cents an hour. I eventually got close - $.25 cents an hour. Guys making that much dough were considered rich.

Having a job afforded me several things. I was allowed to live in a cell. I know that sounds crazy and everyone assumes that all prisoners get a bunk in some sort of cell. But if you don't have a job, you sleep on a cot, dormitory style, in an open room; an atrium. Trust me, the cell is better. I got to get outside more because I had to walk to my job. Most of all, I got to occupy my hands and my mind. Work kept me sane. I even volunteered to cut the grass on weekends so I could keep busy and the bonus was the small of that fresh cut grass; something normal, something I would do at my own home. If I closed my eyes when I pushed that mower, I could pretend I was cutting my own lawn, that my kids were playing in the yard, my mom making me lemonade for when the job was done. The only problem was, I had to open my eyes at some point and there was reality.

Once I started working at the prison, it seemed as if the other inmates no longer viewed me as a newbie. I had grown roots. People started opening up to me more and occasionally I saw people with items that weren't sold in the canteen. I figured if I could be known as a guy who could get stuff, I'd be much better protected. I needed to find out how to do that in order to be indispensable to people of all ethnic groups, gangs, and affiliations.

I also got involved in some of the programs they had for inmates and quickly realized that it was mostly for show. Many of the inmates couldn't even read. There was a monotonous routine of programs and services that in reality were designed to keep the inmates under control and occupied instead of helping them. From the inside, I saw the prison system as a political profit center for the first time. However, some civil servants I met were genuinely involved in helping the inmates cope with the harsh environments we lived in.

I decided that, from the inside, I could do more help than those on the outside so I started to teach some of the inmates how to read. By doing so, I started to become better treated by the guards, because they saw me as a decent guy, but also I became more valuable to some of the inmates, which meant less people were willing to fuck with me.

Still, I lived in hell. One morning I woke up as usual to go to breakfast and when I began to put on my boots I felt something warm and wet inside one of them. Someone had just pissed in my boots. On another occasion, as I reached out to turn on my radio and listen to some news from the outside before going to sleep, it was missing. Someone had stolen it.

I had also learned early on to wait until the last minute to get to the chow line. Getting there late meant you had very little time to eat and had to eat fast, but it was better than going early. I had gone there early a few times only to have the prison goons, people that nightmares were made out of, take my food right from my tray. These were people that would rather kill you than laugh with you and prison food was not worth my life.

I met Rae Carruth in the prison. He was a former professional football player, who played wide receiver for the Carolina Panthers of the NFL. In 2001 he was found guilty of conspiring to murder a woman who was pregnant with his child. It never ceased to amaze me how so many people "find God" in prison. As for Rae, he became a Muslim. While he was a physical freak, he was very laid back and quite peaceful. He was also the fastest human being I ever saw with my own two eyes. Once, we were able to play a softball tournament in the yard and he was so fast that he could play left field and catch a ball that was hit to the right side of the field. Watching him race around the bases is a memory still etched in my mind.

However, not even Rae got a free pass from all the prisoners. On one occasion, someone disrespected him and tried to steal from him. Ray beat the shit out of that guy something fierce. When the correction officers came, they didn't do anything to Rae, but the other guy got sent to the hole. We all knew when Rae would have a court date because there would be helicopters hovering around the prison. I guess they were trying to get video or an image of him shackled and in his prison clothes.

I also met best-selling author Michael Peterson. He is an American novelist who was convicted of murdering his second wife. He was the true definition of an introvert, a recluse. He would rarely come out of his cell. Whenever I would see him he would either be writing or reading, even in the chow hall. He was not nearly as imposing a figure as Rae was but still, I didn't see anyone mess with him. I figured he was getting stuff from the outside. In prison no one gets a free ride. You either join a gang and they make you do shit, or if you're solo, you have to find a way to be valuable. Michael's case got overturned in 2011.

Jail was every bit as hellacious as I thought it would be. I was once told that if someone ever placed an object inside of your pockets at the food line, your best bet was to act as if they didn't. Someone else would eventually reach into your pocket and get it out. Gangs and goons used people like that to carry illegal shit all the time. If you reacted at all and brought attention to yourself, your very life would be in danger. I actually saw someone get stabbed in front of me for that very reason. This happened to me on several occasions early on. I would pray that whoever was supposed to get it out of my pockets would come quickly and not get us both caught. I knew I had to make alliances or something stupid could happen and my sentence could be extended, or I could be killed. It was an animal farm in there, a wild and dangerous place fraught with monsters.

* * * *

"How do people get stuff in here?" I asked Oz, one of the most popular rednecks, for about the hundredth time. He was a short skinny white guy with long blonde hair, red goatee, and tons of tats, but no muscle. However, no one messed with him because he was one of the guys that could procure items from the outside. When I had asked the first few times, he told me that no one would tell me anything until I had proved myself to be able to keep my mouth shut. Now that some time had passed and I had seen things, and had experienced violence myself and not told on anyone, I figured I might be able to finally get an answer.

Oz was pensive for a few moments before he answered in his half southern/half Irish redneck slang. "There be a guard dat help out wit dat. S'up to him if he eva let you know who he be. I'll get word to him but it gone costchu." I paid Oz with stamps to pass on the word for me.

Since prison is a cashless society, we used the canteen items as currency. You could get people do to just about anything for stamps, cigarettes, candy bars, coffee, books, skin magazines, wool socks, or soup. Out of everything in there though, stamps and cigarettes held the most value. The reason why stamps were so valuable was because they found a way to turn them into currency. Inmates would mail the stamps to a trusted person on the outside who would go to the post office and sell the stamps back to them for money. They would then take that money and deposit it into their accounts, which enabled them to buy whatever they wanted from the canteen.

Everyone had an ID card with a magnetic strip in the back that you would give to the canteen clerk/officer to swipe. You would have to have family or friends deposit money into your account, which would be synced up to your ID card. Some had been there so long that their family and friends stopped putting money in their accounts, but most of the others never had someone put money in there in the first place. My advantage was that I had money and most of the people in there didn't.

About a week later, Oz approached me. "He said he give you a shot but don't think you gone meet'em. I'm bout to getchu an address, can't write shit down tho, need to keep it in ya head. Someone from out need ta put dat papah and a list to dat address." He looked around and got a little closer to me and told me the address to a PO box. "Whatchu lookin' to get anywayz? He aint gone bring big shit in here, nah mean?"

"I need teeth whitening strips, a pair of sunglasses, two Timex watches, and supplements."

"Whatchu mean supple-mints?" he asked in his heavy southern drawl.

"GNC grade fat-burning stuff." He looked at me with a blank expression. "Work out shit from the GNC store," I said. I had made friends with some murderers by working out with them on what was called the pile, short for the weight pile.

"He might be able to git all dat. It don't all come at once. Gottsta tip da man though. $20 or $30 be nuff. Aint worf it t' fuck around and be cheap, if'n so he jess keep dat papah and yo ass won't get shit."

Oz was right. It took a while for my first order of supplies to trickle in. I told my connection outside, my mom, to give him a $100 tip. I wanted him to put my orders at the front of the line. I secured my value to the weight lifting murderers, which consequently bought me protection from anyone who would want to hurt me. I did about four orders through the anonymous corrections officer, each time giving him an extra $100, before he let me meet him.

He approached me and let me know that he was the guy smuggling the stuff in for me. I knew who he was. The prisoners had a name for him, Mack Truck, but I had never spoken to him before. Although he tried to downplay it, he let me know that he appreciated the $100 tips. Being a former pilot had its privileges in prison when it came to finances.

Mack and I began to chat on a regular basis, although I never gave him my order in person. After several more runs, he agreed to meet my mother and sister on the outside. Eventually he would meet them at a Wal-Mart and they would just hand him the items along with his tip. At times it would take him a month to bring everything in. He would deliver one watch, then whenever he was comfortable he would smuggle in two baggies filled with the GNC powder, and so on and so forth. The guards never got searched as far as I knew, so he would sneak items in his shoe or wherever he felt was the safest place. He would never personally deliver it to me, either. I would come into my cell to find an item under my pillow. That's how I knew it had arrived.

I had found a way to protect myself from a fight on the inside. On the outside however, I wanted to take on the entire North Carolina justice system. I was itching for a fight. I kept remembering a part of the movie, Tombstone, when they used the verse in Revelation 6:8: "I looked, and behold, a pale horse! And its rider's name was Death, and Hell rode with him . . ."

I wanted to be that rider and bring all of Hell's fury to Judge Hill.

Chapter 12

Larry's Brilliant Idea

It felt like Christmas when I could receive visitors a few days after being sent to Nash County Jail. It had been almost two months since I had been sentenced and I hadn't been able to hug any visitors since. When my mother and sister came to visit me, my emotions got the best of me and I just let it all out. I cried about losing my dad and me not being able to be there to support my mom and family throughout that difficult time. I cried because I had not held my sons in months and I wondered how they were doing. I also cried because even though I had been hit, smacked, spit on, and mistreated, I knew that the worst was still to come. My mother held me while my sister hugged us both as the three of us cried together. I could not express in words how grateful I was that they were there.

Larry also came to see me. I knew he would come eventually, but I wasn't sure what to tell him. I never told him about being charged with rape. I had just told him that I needed to go to North Carolina and take care of a personal matter. Larry was so cool with me that he actually bought me the plane ticket that got me to my trial. Being that I was sure I would beat the charge, I had asked him to get me a round trip ticket.

The day I had been found guilty, my buddy Erik, who had been my flight instructor and helped me get a job at Colgan Air, called him and told him what had happened. Larry quickly called my mom and asked for every single detail of the case and of my predicament. As soon as I could receive visitors, Larry flew up to see me. My mom picked him up at the airport and brought him to the prison.

"How are you doing?" Larry asked. picking up the phone and looking at me through the thick glass window at the jail's visiting room. "I only have 10 minutes, but I want you to know I'm here for you and I'm going to give it all I have to get you out of here."

When he hung up and gestured a silent good bye, I noticed tears in his eyes, together with the determined look of a man who has just made a solemn oath. And so he did. Larry immediately wrote a letter to Bruce Cunningham, my appellate attorney, to establish my character and vouch for my professional and moral integrity. Part of Larry's letter reads:

> *Aside from business and speaking as a father of two grown children, I must say that there could not be a more loving, nurturing, and dedicated father to be found than Will Smith. The consistency of*

his gentle demeanor and caring personality are reflected in the faces of his two sons, which is a source of joy to all those around them.

And Larry didn't stop there. He stayed close to mom and continued to visit me in jail every month.

"I have to do something, bro. I can't be at peace knowing you're in here," he said to me during one of his first visits. We had only worked together for four months but in that short time we had developed a close friendship as well as a great working relationship.

I felt sad to let him down, but happy to know that he valued me as much as he did. Once a month he would fly up from Tampa, get picked up by my mother, and get back on an airplane later that day, just to see me in person for a few minutes. As time went on, I would call him a lot and share with him the bullshit I was living with. In one particular visit, he had a different kind of look, as if he was up to something.

"Will, I thought of something on the flight up here today. I want you to hear me out, okay?"

"Sure, what the fuck else do I have to do?" I said into the phone.

"How about if we put up a website and let the world know what a piece of shit Judge Hill really is?"

"I don't think I'm getting what you're saying Larry. What do you mean?"

"That bitch fucked you over and hardly anyone knows about it. But I tell you what, if she did that to you, a fucking pilot for a major airline, I bet you she screwed over a ton of other people that aren't nearly as well off as you were. The world needs to know of the abuse and wrongdoings of this bitch." He switched the phone to his left hand and a smirk edged his lips. "Basically, I want your permission to publicly trash her and see if we can illicit comments from others. She can't just get away with what she did to you!"

"Fuck it man. Let's do it," I said, "What else can she do to me, right?"

The next few times I talked to Larry on the phone, we got serious about creating the website. We had thought to call it *Eradicate Evelyn Hill*, but we were going to spell Evelyn *Evil-yn*. Some people I mentioned it to advised me not to do it, that there was no good that could come of it for me. However, I wanted her to know that, in my own way, I was fighting back.

The next time Larry came to visit me, he had printed out a bunch of pictures of Judge Hill from different articles. He had even distorted her face on some of the images and made her appear as an evil ugly witch. He also brought with him a slew of facts from some of the cases she had presided over. We laughed as we figured out the final details of how the site was going to look and what our message was going to be.

A couple of weeks later, I was on the phone with Larry and we were ready to launch the site. He had sent me printouts of what the site was going to look like and I made recommendations and he made edits until we got it to look the way we wanted it to. George Hughes, my trial attorney, also got involved. He gave Larry the email addresses of all of the lawyers that he knew. Because she was a circuit judge, she had presided over cases for many attorneys all across the state of North Carolina. We hoped that there would be at least one or two that were bold enough to say something about an active judge.

"Okay, Will, it's all set." Larry said to me over the phone. "Are you really ready for this?"

"You bet your ass I'm am." I had been teaching inmates to write, and how to fight for themselves by setting up appeals and sending out letters. There was no way I could go down without a fight. "Did you contact the newspapers?"

"I contacted a few, but I don't know if it will do anything." Larry answered. "Just say the word, Will, and I'll hit the button. A link to this site is going to go to literally thousands of people. We are about to start a major shit storm. Are you sure you're ready for this?"

"Larry?"

"Yeah?"

"Hit the fucking button."

* * * *

The very next morning, the manager of the pod I was in, Mr. Conn, came to my cell after breakfast with a weird look on his face. "Follow me," he ordered. I followed him

Falling From The Sky

and another corrections officer to a private room. There he handed me a newspaper. He couldn't show favoritism and show me the paper out in the open because inmates were not supposed to see printed materials. As I brought the paper closer, I saw the distorted face of Judge Evelyn Hill in all its ugliness.

Sure enough, the website made the front page of the *Raleigh News and Observer* on its first day!

"You crazy motherfucker!" he said to me in a congratulatory manner. "You are incredible, Smith. I can't believe you did this."

"Well I sure as shit didn't do this alone," I muttered as I tried to read the article. Mr. Conn had the decency of giving me the time to read the article twice before he escorted me to the door.

"I can't wait to see how this is going to play itself out," he said. "Good luck to you, man."

With that, I left the small room and walked back to my cell feeling something I hadn't felt in a long time, a glimmer of hope. As I neared my cell, another guard came to get me for a phone call. It was Bruce, my new attorney. My former attorney, George, was a man of his word. He had told me that he would do anything in his power to help me and he did, he actually hired Bruce for me and paid for him out of his own pocket!

"It's getting an overwhelming response, Will," Bruce said.

"Is that good or bad? I can't tell by your voice."

"Honestly, I don't know. This could go either way. So far it's only you; a convicted rapist versus a sanctioned judge of the court." That was one of the things I liked about Bruce, he always gave it you straight.

"What do I have to lose though, right?"

"Right," he answered. "I'm behind you 100 percent, buddy."

He was, too. Bruce had even help start a program called The North Carolina Center on Actual Innocence. It was designed to give a chance to those who claim they are imprisoned wrongfully, but don't have the finances to fight for themselves. It was he who put together the appellate briefing that was going to be voted on by five judges.

Even though the North Carolina justice system had failed me, it didn't mean that I was going to fail. Although I found myself in the most horrible of places I could imagine, I refused to give up. There was no way that I would live even one day in that jail without fighting to get my freedom back.

What I couldn't have known at the time was the bombardment of phone calls and emails that were made to the Nash County Jail. Journalists, friends, family members of other people that had gotten treated unfairly from Judge Hill, and reporters all wanted to talk to me. In fact, the prison stopped allowing me to take any calls.

The next time I talked to Larry, he told me that we had received an overwhelming response from prior victims of Judge Hill's style of justice. Several families had already posted their stories of her. He did a superb job of running the site. He began to forward the many e-mails we were getting denouncing Judge Hill for her unfair, unethical, and illegal proceedings. The tide had begun to turn, or so I had hoped. But I was still a prisoner who encountered really deranged psychopaths every day.

Another time, when Larry came to see me in person, he told me he and my mother had sent a letter to the governor of North Carolina. I read a copy of the letter and my eyes welled up with tears. I couldn't believe that someone I had just met four months ago would go through the lengths he did to try to get me out.

I didn't know when the appeals committee would look at my case. I found out that they had when I received a letter from them. I opened the letter up in half excitement and half dread. I held the letter open in front of me, but closed my eyes. I took a few long breaths, knowing that whatever this letter contained would be my fate for the foreseeable future. I had been through so much over the last year and another blow could have caused me serious psychological damage. I made a silent prayer and opened my eyes.

The phrase "4-1" was the first thing I focused on. My heart tried to jump out of my mouth and I force myself to read the first paragraph from the beginning. I had won my appeal! The judges ruled 4-1 in my favor!

However, as I read I discovered that because one judge ruled against me, I would have to stay in prison until my case could be reviewed by the Supreme Court of the state of North Carolina. I wasn't out of this hellhole yet. I wasn't even close!

When you are incarcerated, they don't tell you when you are going to go to court. They do this mostly to protect you. For example, if you knew when you were going to court and told someone, they would use that against you and try to take advantage of you. They would try to steal from you or do something to you because they knew that you would most likely not fight back and ruin your chance at getting in front of a judge again.

So, every morning I hoped that one of the guards would tell me to get ready to be transported somewhere. However, as days slowly turned into weeks, I began to fall back into despair. I knew I just had to go to court and I would be free but I didn't know when that would be. So every morning I woke with a glimmer of hope only to have it crash down around me until all hope left me.

Weeks turned into months and I forced myself to not dwell on the looming court date. I found out that at times it took years to get an appeal date. *Years!* This was the toughest time of my incarceration. I still had to put up with a lot of shit and the helplessness of not knowing how long I would be there, even though a piece of paper already stated I was free. It was exasperating. I was still locked up like an animal.

Knowing that I was going to be free one day, though, lit something inside of me to help out some of the inmates even more. I wanted to leave my mark on that place so mired in misery. I started to look over other inmates' cases with them and would even ask George or Bruce questions regarding some of the cases I was trying to help with.

I tried to be a resource to some of the new inmates who came in after me. However, it's not easy to get someone's trust in prison. Unfortunately, some of the newer prisoners had to learn the hard way, either from the guards or from fellow inmates, about how things are done in Nash.

Three months turned into four, and then five and then six. In total I spent another full year in prison, the whole time knowing that I would be freed on my court date. I understood why they wouldn't tell me when my court date was though. If any of the other inmates know that you are about to go to court to possibly be released, that's when they truly start messing with you because they know you won't be inclined to get into a fight and jeopardize your impending freedom.

One fateful morning, a correctional officer that I had never seen before woke me before the sun was up.

"Pack your shit. You're going to court."

Chapter 13

Back to Court - Redemption

"Pack everything you've got and put these on," the guard commanded. I got dressed in the white t-shirt and white pants they gave me and then I put on my black "bobos" (boots). Those were my court clothes.

They transported me to the same courthouse in Wake County, where I had been sentenced 26 months earlier. In fact, they even put me in the same cell I had stayed in. I was there alone for several hours. I had been in jail for more than two years and I was familiar with time going by slowly, however, due to the anticipation I had of possibly being free, the wait seemed like an eternity. My mind started playing tricks on me, I wondered if somehow, some way, I would get screwed over again and get sent back to Nash. I wondered if my family and friends knew I was there. Finally one of the guards grabbed another prisoner from another cell, which indicated to me that it was after 9 a.m. and court was in session. That's when time decided to just sit down and take a nap!

The cell I was placed in had no windows. I was surrounded by walls and a solid steel door with a small window. I lost track of time and must have gone delusional, because at one point I felt like a whole day had gone by.

Anxiety and anticipation don't mix well and when you add desperation to the equation. Your mind starts playing all kinds of tricks on you. Finally, after eating a bland lunch, they came to get me and brought me to the courtroom.

Although there were benches in the holding area for inmates to sit, I was the only one there. I was fed up with feeling and being alone. I was yearning for human company, but company of the good kind, like friends and family. I wanted to feel cherished, and loved, and appreciated, and respected, just like any other decent person would.

"You're that pilot aren't you?" the bailiff asked,

"Yes."

"You're the one that got Judge Hill thrown out right?"

"Yes."

"I want to shake your hand," he continued. He approached me and extended his hand, which I met with a firm handshake. "That's the best thing that could have happened to the state of North Carolina." He left the room only to return in a few minutes to escort me into the courtroom.

Time to Shine

"Okay, Mr. Smith, now is your time to shine," the bailiff said as he escorted me out of the holding area and into the courtroom.

I entered the courtroom with no shackles or handcuffs. That was a good feeling. As I looked around, I saw my good friend and student, Nathan Wright, my mom, my sister, and Larry. I breathed a sigh of relief at the sight of my loved ones.

The State attorney was Jeff Cruden, the same one that had prosecuted me. My lawyer Bruce was busy at another court hearing. We had previously brought on a second counsel named Joseph Cheshire III, a prominent lawyer who sat on the O. J. Simpson case.

"Your honor, the Supreme Court has upheld the appellate court's decision in favor of Mr. William Beach Smith," Joe pleaded. "The time has come for this court to release this man and set him free."

"I think Mr. Smith has learned his lesson," The=DA said as he gave his recommendation for my immediate release. "The state has no objections to his release."

Whatever the DA meant by "learned his lesson" I will probably never find out. But the truth of the matter is that the only ones that had to learn a lesson from my case were the members of the decadent and incompetent judicial system of the state of North Carolina.

"Now what?" I looked at Joe.

"You're going home!" Those were the sweetest words I had heard in a very long time.

I was motioned to go with the bailiffs to get processed out. They ushered me through hallways and corridors and I wound up at the same place where I had surrendered my suit, drivers' license, which hadn't expired, and all my other stuff more than two years earlier. It was all there, I got it all back in a brown paper bag.

I still had a hard time believing all this was happening. I was really being handed my life back. I was about to reenter society. I was finally going to be able to walk, talk, move, and do just about anything I wanted as a free man.

On my way out of the processing center's warehouse, I went by one of the cell blocks where they place incoming detainees. They had brought in a group of girls and placed them in a cell, most probably on prostitution or drug charges. Then all of a sudden, one of them took her top off and pressed her breasts up against the bars.

"Hey, you!" she yelled at me. "Lick my pussy, big boy!" she said as she grabbed her crotch. Immediately, one of the officers saw her and restrained her.

When I was finally released it was about 5 p.m. As they opened the door to a big atrium, many of my friends and family were there waiting for me. I cried tears of joy and hugged everyone. There's no better feeling in the world than hugging and be hugged by someone you love, someone that carries your own blood, someone who is willing to stand by you no matter what.

"What do you want to do, man?" Nate, one of my best friends, asked as I turned around to greet him.

"I want to kiss the first thing outside of the state of North Carolina. I don't care if it's a fucking swamp." We all laughed.

As my heart pounded, my brain drained of all the harshness, anger, fear, and hatred that had become part of me during my incarceration. Before getting in a car and driving as far away from that place as possible, I looked up at the sky and breathed in the freshest air ever. I can still remember the taste of that air.

For more than two years, I had been in a place where the air, the sky, my favorite place in this world, was only accessible to me in small doses. For all those months, I had never been outside at night, to see the stars and the moon. How many times had I flown among those stars, seen that moon from far above the earth? How I had missed the sky after falling so far from it.

I am free now. No shackles and no bars! I yelled the words aloud in my head. I began to smile at life again. I had a euphoric flow of energy coursing through me and couldn't stop talking and thanking everyone for standing with me through thick and thin.

"Let's go to Kanki," I jubilantly exclaimed.

My mother had brought me a change of clothes and I changed in the car and promptly threw away the white clothes and uncomfortable bobos. We laughed all the way to Kanki's, a Japanese place in Raleigh that served the best teppanyaki and sushi. We had a blast! I have never enjoyed sushi as much as I did that day.

After we ate and things finally started to slow down, I realized I had nowhere to live, no car, no money, nothing. I realized I had to sleep somewhere but had no place to stay.

"Larry, I'm going to need a place to stay," I said.

"Come on, Will, my home is your home," he smiled. "You can stay with me for as long as you want."

The celebration lasted well into the night. At some point during our revelry, I realized what I needed to do. My path was clear. I didn't know what I would do for a living, but I did know where I needed to be.

The next morning I called Tracey. "I'm coming home to see my boys. She couldn't believe it. She cried. I got on the next plane to Florida. Words can't express the joy I felt when I saw those two smiling faces again. For the first time in a long time, I felt whole, complete. I was back to being the thing that gave me the most pleasure. I was a father again.

Chapter 14

Emotional Meltdown

My induction back into society was not an easy task. In fact, it was a long and painful process. The psychological scars inflicted on my persona by the prison system were deep and hard to heal. I suffered from night terrors for a full year. At times I would wake up sweaty and find myself swinging my fists in an effort to protect myself from the visions that tormented me. Other times, I would just wake up in the middle of the night and not know exactly where I was.

People are considered institutionalized if they spend more than 24 months incarcerated. I had adapted to an environment where being paranoid, overly protective of your belongings, and not trusting anyone was vital for survival. Being punched in the face, spat at, threatened, used, and stolen from are the materials in which walls are built that are hard to destroy.

I didn't realize I was doing it, but I was looking at people, even some people that I knew had my back, trying to find out how they were going to try to screw me over. I would stay awake at night trying to figure out what their angle was, how they were going to try to steal from me or exploit me.

There were also some "respects" you learn to adhere to in prison that are not applied outside of it. For example, in prison you don't walk up to two people that are engaged in a conversation and interrupt them. The phrase "excuse me" doesn't reduce the insult they feel by your intrusion. Also, if a guy is asleep, you sure as hell don't wake him up to ask him something. You would get the shit smacked out of you. Sleep was a getaway from our reality. I would have preferred to be sleeping and having a nightmare instead of being awake and living in one. Inmates don't have much, so their respect means a lot. When someone felt disrespected, a physical encounter almost always swiftly occurred.

Most times, people wouldn't disrespect someone, because even if they would get the better of a fight, both inmates would go to the hole. So, it wasn't worth it. If someone was going to go to the hole, they were going to deserve it, which is why many of the fights were extremely brutal. Although it sounds weird to some, because the code of conduct is different, people respected each other more in prison. There were times when, as I was trying to adjust back to society, I would feel disrespected according to the prison system. I had to intentionally restrain myself.

"Mom, I feel sad all the time," I confessed after having dinner with my mother. It was about two weeks since I had been released. "It's as if something inside of me had been mutilated."

"Don't focus on those dark times, Will. Those days are over. I don't understand. I think I would be happy if I were you."

"That's just it, mom. I know I should be happy, but instead I'm always angry and jittery."

The whole truth was that I was also afraid. I didn't know why. I knew I was safe from the people I had done time with. Still I couldn't find any peace, and I couldn't find a good groove.

"When I was in there I would daydream of eating real good food again, like your food."

She smiled at me briefly. I could always get her to smile by complimenting her as a cook, but then her smile faded and her eyebrows scrunched up as she looked intently at me. "And although the food is every bit as good as I remember, I'm not eating well."

I was in an emotional crisis. I knew something was wrong, but I didn't know the terminology for what it was. I didn't want to say too much to my family and friends who had supported me throughout my ordeal, so I was trying to just deal with it by myself and I was realizing that I couldn't. The turmoil inside of me was becoming unbearable.

Days later, I confided in my friend Larry. I think he understood me a little more than my mother. As a parent, when your children are suffering, your feelings get too wrapped up in it to look at things objectively at times. When I told him that I felt like a pressure cooker about to explode, he told me he knew how to help. The next morning, Larry called to give me the name of a well-known clinical psychologist. He recommended him for his ability to deal with ex-convict's traumatic syndromes.

"Dr. William Longletter can help, Will. He specializes in helping ex-convicts regain their sense of dignity," he told me. I cringed at being called an ex-convict, but that was my life, whether it was fair or not. I called his office and made an appointment immediately after Larry gave me his number.

A few days later I sat in Dr. Longletter's waiting room. I actually learned quite a lot while I was there as I read some white papers. I realized that it was very common for ex-convicts to find it a difficult process when re-entering society. I read an article on what it takes to break the cycle of criminal life and incarceration and realized that although my case got overturned and I wasn't a "criminal," I had learned how to live like one during the years that I lived with them. I read true accounts of individuals who got released and exhibited a pattern of destructive behavior that they had never displayed before. The people that typically got hurt the most were the families, the children in particular.

I closed my eyes and swore to myself that I would not let the last two years of my life ruin my relationship with my kids or their future.

"Mr. Smith, Dr. Longletter will see you now," a blonde-haired secretary with a great smile said to me.

I met Dr. Longletter with a smile and a firm handshake. We began with some small talk and I couldn't help but feel a spark of hope. I sensed that the good doctor was an intelligent individual. As we spoke, I discovered that he was passionate about helping others recover from traumatic and crippling experiences, some caused by life-threatening situations or prolonged exposure to extreme hardship. I qualified under both.

As expected, the doctor asked me a lot of questions and limited his interruptions as I answered, at length, as honestly as I could. During the following 45 minutes, I knew I was being carefully studied and observed by a professional psychoanalyst. Towards the end of our time, he looked up from jotting something down in my folder, smiled, and shared with me the process he was going to take me through.

"Mr. Smith, during the next several weeks, we are going to work together to help you regain the sense of direction and self-worth that was almost completely taken from you during your exposure to the destructive influences of the criminal incarceration system."

When I left the doctor's office with another appointment set, I felt a slight relief from the deep depression that was affecting my psyche. But still, my reality was far from encouraging. Just as it's true that time heals everything, sometimes the labels that we have been branded with remain etched in our soul much longer than we would care to admit.

Against the World

The best part of my situation was that I was not alone. My family was extremely helpful and sensitive to what I was going through. My friends also rose the occasion and cheered me up whenever they could. The therapy sessions that followed also proved to be very helpful. Dr. Longletter helped me identify those areas in my life that needed attention. He guided me on how to establish a set of priorities that proved invaluable to my recovery.

I had been out of jail for two months and just as I started to get into a bit of a groove, although I still had nightmares, Larry handed me an official letter when I got to his house. It was from the Raleigh Police Department. With a sigh, I opened it and, after reading it, immediately called my lawyer.

"George," I blurted out as soon as he answered. "I just got a letter from Raleigh PD. They say that I have to register as a sex offender!"

"Slow down, Will," George said. His voice always had a way of calming me down. "Calm down and read the letter to me."

I read him the letter and then we didn't say anything for several moments. I knew George was running a bunch of different solutions in his head and didn't want to interrupt his thoughts. Finally I said, "If I fail to register as a sex offender in the state of North Carolina, I would commit a Class F felony! There's no way in hell I'm going for this George. We have to do something."

"Sex offender registry requirements vary by state, Will, although they share basic characteristics. I'll look into it and see what I can do."

"Thanks George but..."I hated being in a situation when I needed help but had no resources to pay for it. I had just about bankrupted myself in trying to win my case, and since my release I hadn't been able to earn much. My voice nearly cracked as I said, "I can't pay your rate at this time. But I just can't live with that stigma following me around for the rest of my life. I don't know what to do."

"Don't worry about it, Will. You paid me in full before and I wasn't able to fully represent you. After all the hell you went through, this one is on me."

Sex offenders are legally required to live far from children. Many reside in cars, under overpasses, in the woods, or wherever they can live in hiding. It is not uncommon for some to become recluses, rejects of society. They seldom find gainful employment because there is no legal statute that says an employer should show leniency in hiring a registered sex offender. They are also unable to use any mind- or mood-altering substances, such as alcohol. I was pissed that they would force me to live such a difficult lifestyle based on a charge that I was ultimately found innocent of.

George did everything he could within the confines of the laws of the state of North Carolina, but there was no way around it. If I stayed there, I had to register as a sex offender. George, my mother, Larry, and I had a conversation and set a plan in motion for me to move out of North Carolina. George had arranged it so that I could move to Florida and not have to register as a sex offender and Larry had agreed to take me in until I got back on my feet.

George brought me to the Greyhound station on the last day of my residency in the state of North Carolina. We had a heart-to-heart conversation and he made me promise him that I would put all the crap that I had endured behind me and focus on building my life again.

I used the 23-hour bus trip from Raleigh to Tampa to readjust my way of thinking. Although I didn't realize it, I had let what had happened to me eat away at the optimism I had once had in my life. While I was in prison, I lost not only my father but my beloved grandmother and my dear brother-in-law. I couldn't mourn them or show any remorse, sadness of for that matter humanity. Emotions like that could cost you in prison. Any sign of weakness brings out the wolves who smell it and use it against you. I had a lot to let go of and it was going to take some time to retrain my mind and regain my footing. .

Sure, what I went through was utter bullshit, but there was no way I could let that play into my future. I thought of Evelyn Hill, Jill, the trial, the crazy things I saw in prison, the horrible things I endured, and savored it all. I had to internalize everything in a whole new way. It could no longer be the reason why things would go wrong for me. I had to turn those things into the reason why I was going to make things right.

When I arrived at the bus station in downtown Tampa, Larry and my mother were waiting for me with open arms. I inhaled the Tampa air and realized that I was home. As we drove to Larry's house I smiled, because for the first time in a long time, I felt free.

Epilogue

The Judicial Standards Committee of North Carolina publicly reprimanded Judge Evelyn Hill. February of 2006 she was forced to step down from the bench. She was told she could never run as an elected official or practice law ever again. In addition, popular protests demanded her retirement pension be cut in half.

Our judicial system failed me, however, that does not mean that I lived the rest of my life as a victim. I was far from being beaten by the raw deal that was dealt me. Due to the wrongful imprisonment I suffered, and as the popularity of my appeal became evident, more than 28 cases of abusive and illegal prosecution from the bench of Judge Hill were revised and the innocent were released. Never in the history of the judicial system in the state of North Carolina had such a blatant disregard for justice been sustained for so long by one of the offices of the land that is supposed to uphold the rights guaranteed to all Americans for a just and fair trial. Efforts have been made and measures have been implemented to ensure that such an injustice never repeats itself.

The reality is that our judicial system doesn't work as well as most would like to think. The United States of America is still the best country on the planet. However, we are still flawed. It has been proven over and over again that, at times, our law enforcement has cast wide nets and whoever gets caught up in one is in peril. We preach that we are innocent until proven guilty, but once a charge is placed on someone, everyone looks at him or her as guilty, at times, even once they prove their innocence. The scenario goes like this: officers want to be detectives, and detectives want to be police chiefs. On the other side we have lawyers who want to be assistant DAs. Assistant DAs want to be DAs. DAs want to be judges. Judges want to be senators, and having a high conviction rate is one of the ways to get them there.

In the case of rape accusation, the stigma can last for someone's entire life. What many people don't realize is that many women have accused someone of rape just to feed into their vindictiveness. By law, even without a shred of evidence, you get arrested for rape and forever be labeled by it. The grand jury is nothing but a rubber stamp.

I wish our society were different. I wish we didn't sensationalize unsubstantiated accusations. I had a naked woman in my bed and reacted like most single men would and it ruined my life. In this society, you can say whatever you want and ruin someone, regardless of their past. I didn't have a criminal record. I always did everything above board. I was a helpful and contributing member to society. Yet, I still didn't stand a chance against this broken system.

* * * *

I had no idea how hard it would be to get a good job. Even though I wasn't a registered sex offender, every good job I applied to denied me once they ran a background check. The world kept trying to beat me down and force me to eat crow. However, there was no quit in me.

I was not about to play that little violin and live the rest of my life throwing a pity party. I knew too many people that had succumbed to society's view of them, I couldn't let that happen to me. Just because I got screwed over by the North Carolina Judicial System didn't mean that anyone owed me anything. People might feel sorry for me but no one was going to hand me a hundred grand to get my life together. What I went through definitely hurt me, but I sure as hell wasn't going to let it beat me.

I finally got a job as an exterminator. I had fallen a long way from being a pilot for American Airlines, a long way from the sky, to earning $10 per hour working as an exterminator in the Florida heat. Still, each day, I woke up and tried to be the best exterminator I could be. The biggest obstacle people face is themselves. If they don't have their dream job, they don't try hard. I knew that in order for me to advance, I had to work hard and be the best employee I could be.

I also focused on being the best father I could be. I was determined to make up for lost time. What I went through could not be the story that my kids new about their Dad's life. There had to be more.

Eventually I started my own exterminating company, and with sweat equity and by delivering good service, my business started to flourish. Then I got my pilots license again. Today I smile every time I find myself among the clouds as I fly to Aruba, The Keyes, Barbados, Miami, or some other destination. It wasn't easy. In fact, getting my life back to where it was turned out to be harder than going to prison. I literally went through hell on earth twice, once in prison and the second time as I fought to get my life back on track. I learned a lot about myself and of the power of resiliency.

Today I get called to speak at business events as a motivational speaker and I'm working on being able to get back inside the prison walls to talk to inmates that are soon to be released. I plan to tell them how I overcame the stigma, shame, and un-welcome embrace of society.

I would like to tell you all of it but that is a story for another time.

"This is Captain Will Smith, over and out."

Acknowledgements:

- *To my Mother for standing behind me*
- *To my Father – I wish that I had a chance to say goodbye*
- *To my boys Will and Giff for all their love*
- *To Ericka for accepting me for who I am and never judging me*
- *And to Eli Gonzalez and Lil Barcaski of The Ghost Publishing for bringing all this together*

I love you all!

A Note From the Author:

I would like to thank you for reading my book, it took me over ten years to decide to write this book. I wanted to use the book to be able to reach out to those that have been through the same as I and are looking for a way to rebound from the past into the future. My second book will be on HOW. The struggle is long and hard. However it can be attained.

I have learned that nothing can be done overnight, but hard work and focus will allow anyone to concur and prevail. My experience and my success was through hard work and persistence. Nothing was given to me except trust and respect by the way of honesty and consistency in my works and convictions to accomplishing my goals.

Please enjoy this story of success, and pass it on to anyone that you think has been through something similar

Captain Will Smith

www.ingramcontent.com/pod-product-compliance
Lightning Source LLC
Chambersburg PA
CBHW071210070526
44584CB00019B/2982